A PAST and PRESENT Companion

125 years of
The Helston Railway
1887-2012

By the same author

London Transport Railways Album

Western Region in the 1960s

This is the Southern Region: Central Division

BR Diary 1968-1977

125 years of
The Helston Railway
1887-2012

Chris Heaps LL.B, FCILT

Past & Present Publishing Ltd

First published in 2012

British Library Cataloguing in Publication Data

A catalogue record for this book is available from the British Library.

ISBN 978 1 85895 277 2

Subscribers' edition 978 1 85895 281 9

Past & Present Publishing Ltd
The Trundle
Ringstead Road
Great Addington
Kettering
Northants NN14 4BW

Tel/Fax: 01536 330588
email: sales@nostalgiacollection.com
Website: www.nostalgiacollection.com

Printed and bound in the Czech Republic

All tickets and labels are from the author's collection.

Title page: The Common Seal of the Helston Railway Company is very similar to the seal of the Borough of Helston itself. It portrays St Michael, the patron saint of the town, slaying the Devil and saving the town. The Archangel Michael is said to have killed the Devil with a 'great slab of stone which was reputed to be nothing less than the veritable lid of Hell, the Hell Stone after which the town had been named'. This stone lay in the entrance to the Angel Hotel and was formerly one of the sights of the town. Sadly, it was split in two in 1783 but can still be seen on either side of a window in the building. The Angel Hotel was formerly the town house of the Earls of Godolphin. *Helston Museum*

Contents

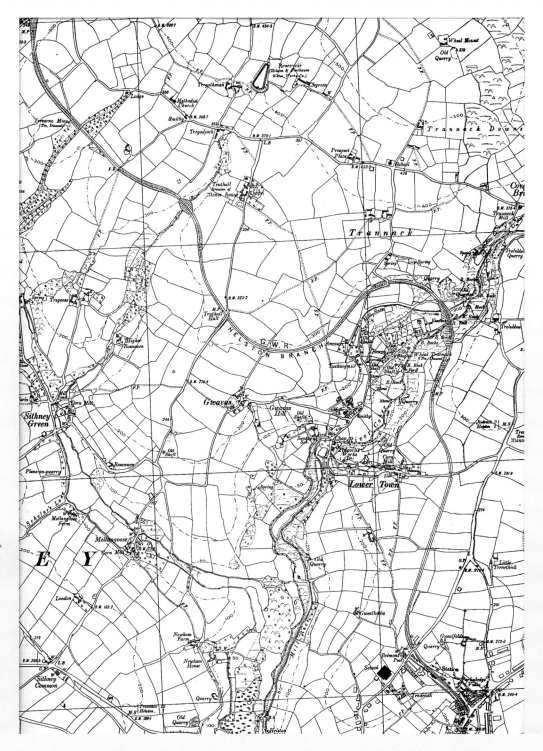

A 1906 map showing the lower part of the Helston branch, from Prospidnick Bridge across the minor road from Sithney to Wendron near Chynhale (top left), through Truthall Halt (left of centre), the horseshoe curve over Cober Viaduct, and Helston station (bottom right). *Crown Copyright*

That Helston (Cornwall) was not a negligible place as long ago as the 11th century is shown by an entry in the Exeter Domesday that Earl Harold held the manor when Edward the Confessor died, while it was among the earliest of English towns to become a borough when it received its first charter from King John on 15 April 1201. More than 800 years later it still remains the market town and focal point of the Lizard peninsula.

Helston is famous not only within the United Kingdom but throughout the world for its annual Furry Dance, which takes place on 8 May (or on the nearest Saturday if that date falls on a Sunday or Monday). Residents dance behind the Helston Town Band through the streets and in and out of houses and shops to welcome the spring. This ancient festival, believed to be pre-Christian, not only survives but has flourished during the last 100 years, and has become even better known by various renditions of the tune. These range from the Edwardian-style song 'The Floral Dance', written by Katie Moss in 1911, and made famous by numerous performances and records by the baritone Peter Dawson, to a very attractive if inaccurate version by the Brighouse & Rastrick Band, which held the No 2 position in the charts for nine weeks in 1977. This ancient festival, unlike so many 'traditions', has not had to be revived, but has continuously been enjoyed and supported by Helstonians for many centuries.

To transport enthusiasts, Helston has other grounds for fame. Helston station had the distinction of being the most southerly point of any railway in the United Kingdom, while it is also famous for being the starting point of the first railway-operated motor omnibus service in Great Britain, introduced by the Great Western Railway (GWR) in 1903 to link Helston with The Lizard, Great Britain's most southerly point.

I am fortunate to have close links not only with Helston but also with its railway. I was born in the town, where the maternal side of my family has lived since at least the 19th century, and where I have retained a property. As a young child I spent many hours being entertained by visits to the station. I have been honoured not only by being invited to take part in the Mid-Day Furry Dance over many years, and to lead the dance in 1969, but also by having been appointed as one of the Stewards who organise Flora Day.

The Furry Dance may be of Celtic origin, but it was later adopted by the Christian church and is celebrated on the Feast of St Michael, Helston's patron saint. In the 19th century it comprised two dances. The first was at 7.00am or thereabouts, when the servants could dance before attending upon their masters and mistresses for the rest of the day. The principal dance of the day was at Mid-Day in which the local gentry, their house guests and professional people of the town were invited to take part. After many servants and members of the gentry had been killed in the First World War, it looked as if this ancient festival might die out, and I probably owe my current links with Furry Day to the fact that my great uncle, Jack Rosewarne, was instrumental in introducing a new dance for local children in 1922. Then, about 60 children took part – in 2011 more than 1,200 children aged between 7 and 18 from schools in Helston danced through the streets behind the Helston Town Band.

So far as the Helston Railway is concerned, my great-great-grandfather not only attended the ceremony marking the cutting of the first sod in 1882 but also travelled on the official train celebrating the opening of the line in 1887. I had the more dubious privilege of travelling on the last passenger train in 1962, and later of travelling in the cab of the locomotive hauling one of the twice-daily goods services that survived until October 1964. To mark the demise of the branch, I wrote an article about it that was published in *Railway World* in the following month. More recently, I have had the pleasure of being made the Vice-President of the Helston Railway Preservation Society, which has reopened about a mile of the branch and has plans for its future as a tourist attraction. Trains on the main line at Gwinear Road are operated by First Great Western, and I can therefore claim a further link with the branch, having been appointed as a member of the First Great Western Advisory Board in 2009.

I have also been fortunate in having had links with buses in Helston, having been appointed as the Traffic Commissioner for the Western Traffic Area in 1997, responsible for the regulation of the bus, coach and lorry industries. As part of a dinner speech given in Plymouth in 1997 I expressed my hope that the centenary of the Helston-Lizard motor bus service would be celebrated in appropriate style, as the 75th anniversary had been marked by the Western National Omnibus Company in 1978. The local operators – First Western National, Western Greyhound and Truronian – accepted my challenge with enthusiasm and, although by then the Traffic Commissioner for the Metropolitan & South

Helston is famous worldwide for its ancient Furry Dance (often wrongly referred to as the Floral Dance), the origins of which are claimed by some to be linked to St Michael's victory over the Devil. According to James Dryden Hosken (1931), '…such was the joy of the good folk of Helston at the success of their patron saint that they spontaneously invented the Furry dance and tune there and then, and danced joyously through the houses and streets of the town.' Others say that the dance is the successor of a Celtic fertility ceremony welcoming the spring. Whatever, its origins are lost in the mists of time. Helstonians still celebrate on 8 May each year, and in this photograph the author is shown (third right) dancing with his younger daughter in the Mid-day Dance in 1996 behind David Harris MP, who represented the constituency between 1983 and 1997. There are four dances during the day: at 07.00 and 17.00 (formerly the Servants' Dance); at 09.40 the Children's Dance; and the Mid-Day Dance. Each dance takes place through the streets and houses over a route of at least 3½ miles.

Eastern Traffic Area, I was proud to be the Patron of the committee that organised the celebrations in 2003, referred to later in this book.

May 2012 was the 125th anniversary of the opening of the Helston Railway, and it was fitting that this book should be published not only to mark that important date in the history of the town but also to celebrate the re-commencement of passenger services (albeit limited) on part of the branch.

I have made every effort to ensure accuracy and to attribute images to the appropriate photographers, but I apologise for any errors or omissions. If there are any, they will be my responsibility and they cannot be attributed to any of the people who have given me so much help. I would like to thank in particular Martin Matthews and Janet Spargo of Helston Museum, Peter Treloar, Alan Bennett, Peter Bickford-Smith, David Collings, Colin Billington, Peter J. Kelley, Victor Menhennet, the staff at the Cornish Studies Library, and the officers of the Helston Railway Preservation Society for their support throughout.

Chris Heaps
Helston

More than 1,000 schoolchildren from Helston schools aged between about 7 and 18 years old now take part in the Children's Dance. In the gloriously sunny weather with which Flora Day is so often favoured, cheerful young couples approach the end of the dance in Coinagehall Street in 2010. *Keith Richards*

When the Helston Railway opened to Helston in 1887, this ancient borough celebrated its belated link to a national railway system that had developed so dramatically since the opening of the Stockton & Darlington Railway in 1825 and the Liverpool & Manchester Railway in 1830. It might have been so different, because plans were prepared only a few years after those events for the construction of a railway line that would have come close to Helston. As early as 1834 a Bill had been submitted to Parliament seeking authority for 'making and maintaining a Railway from Hayle in the parish of St Erth in the County of Cornwall to Tresavean Mine in the Parish of Gwennap in the said County, with several Branches therefrom'. The Hayle Railway believed that such a line would be the

'...means of opening and more easy and commodious communication between the Interior of the principal Mining District of the County of Cornwall and the various Shipping Places at Hayle, Portreath and Restrongett [sic] Creek ... and would otherwise be of great public utility.'

One of the branches referred to would diverge from the main line

'...at or near the village of Angarrack and to be made or carried and to pass through or by the mines of Herland, Binner Downs, Wheal Strawberry, Godolphin and Wheal Vor, and to communicate with and terminate at the High Road leading from Hayle to the Borough of Helleston [sic] at or near the point at which the said High Road passes from the Parish of Breage into the Parish of Sithney.'

This terminus would have been only about 3 miles from Helston, albeit on the other side of the Cober valley, and had the line been built it would no doubt have been extended to Helston. The Hayle Railway Act received Royal Assent in 1834 (4 & 5 William IV c118), in the year before the passage of the Great Western Railway Act 1835! However, plans for the branch towards Helston were omitted from the subsequent Act of Parliament obtained in the following year.

In 1846, during the period of the 'Railway Mania', plans were deposited for a line from Helston to Penryn via Gwealmayo, Gweek, Constantine and Mabe. These proposals gained insufficient financial support and failed, although not before some Helstonians had incurred costs for surveying and the Parliamentary application. In 1851 another company opened Wheal Vor, which had closed in the meantime, and Henry Spencer Toy states in his detailed *History of Helston*, published by Oxford University Press in 1936, that in the following year a new route was surveyed from Hayle to Godolphin and Wheal Vor and thence to Helston. The mine was again unsuccessful and the project was dropped.

Following extensive (but abortive) plans at the beginning of the 1860s for railways from Helston to Penryn (via Gweek), and from Helston to Penzance, proposed by the Cornwall Union Railway, the Penryn scheme was again taken up by local landowners – John St Aubyn, John Rogers, Morley Grylls, John Kendall and Alfred Jenkin – and Royal Assent for the Helston & Penryn Junction Railway Act 1864 was obtained on 14

ANNO VICESIMO SEPTIMO & VICESIMO OCTAVO

VICTORIÆ REGINÆ.

****

Cap. cxcvii.

An Act for making a Railway from *Helston* to *Penryn* in the County of *Cornwall*; and for other Purposes.   [14th *July* 1864.]

WHEREAS the Construction of a Railway from the Borough of *Helston* to the *Cornwall* Railway at *Penryn* in the Parish of *Saint Gluvias* in the County of *Cornwall* would be of public and local Advantage: And whereas the Persons herein-after named, together with other Persons, are willing to construct the said Railway, and it is expedient they should be incorporated into a Company for the Purpose of carrying such Undertaking into execution: And whereas it is expedient that the Company so to be incorporated and the *Cornwall* Railway Company should be empowered to make and carry into effect such Arrangements as are herein-after provided with respect to the Railway and Works by this Act authorized to be constructed: And whereas the several Purposes aforesaid cannot be effected without the Authority of Parliament: May it therefore please Your Majesty that it may be enacted; and be it enacted by the Queen's most Excellent Majesty, by and with the Advice and Consent of the Lords Spiritual and Temporal, and Commons, in this present Parliament assembled, and by the Authority of the same, as follows ; (that is to say,)

[*Local.*]   31 E   1. "The

The Helston & Penryn Junction Railway Act 1864.

July 1864 (27 & 28 Vic c197). This Act authorised the raising of £100,000 capital and loans of up to £40,000 to build a broad gauge line 9¾ miles in length from Helston to terminate by a junction with the (broad gauge) Cornwall Railway in the borough of Penryn and Parish of St Gluvias. The Cornwall Railway had opened its extension from Truro to Falmouth via Penryn in August 1863.

This line was again planned via Gweek and Constantine, but the banking crash of 1866 caused the plan to be abandoned. A further bill deposited in Parliament in 1872 (with the approval of the Cornwall Railway) was no more successful, and on this occasion did not even progress as far as Royal Assent.

In its report of the eventual opening of the line, the *Western Daily Mercury* dated 10 May 1887 also referred to abortive schemes to build railways between Helston and Redruth – which failed because of the anticipated costs of tunnelling – and between Helston and Camborne – which would have involved an expensive viaduct across the Carwinnen valley.

However, Helstonians would not be defeated, despite some local residents having lost money in supporting earlier schemes. In 1879 the Helston Railway Company ('the Company') was formed, with a provisional capital of £70,000 in 3,500 shares each of £20, to construct a railway from Helston to Gwinear Road, a somewhat bleak spot on the former West Cornwall Railway main line between Camborne and Hayle. Interestingly, Gwinear Road is not far from the Angarrack junction contemplated in 1834. A bill was deposited in Parliament in February 1880 and its passage was only slightly delayed by the dissolution of Parliament. Royal Assent was obtained on 9 July 1880. The Helston Railway Act 1880 (43 & 44 Vic c48) ('the Act') authorised the construction of

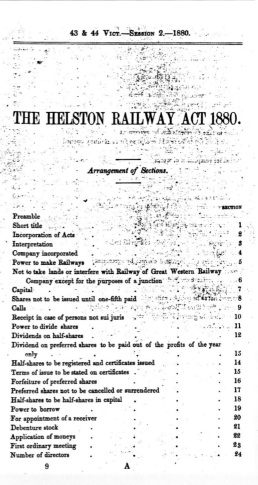

The Helston Railway Act 1880.

'...a Railway eight miles and five furlongs in length commencing by a junction with the West Cornwall Railway of the Great Western Railway on a siding near the Gwinear Road Station thereof in the parish of Gwinear and terminating in the borough and ecclesiastical parish of Helston in a field on the west of the turnpike road or public highway leading from Helston to Redruth.'

The Company had important local support, including the St Aubyn, Bickford Smith and Bolitho families; other well-known local family names referred to in the Act as subscribers included Richard Martyn, Henry Rogers, Robert Cade, J. Walter Tyacke and William Penrose. The original directors were William Bickford Smith JP of Trevarno (Chairman); David Bain JP, banker, of Redruth and Helston; William Bolitho JP, banker, of Penzance and Helston; Richard Martyn JP, Mayor of Helston; Richard Rows of Helston; and W. Molesworth-St Aubyn MP. This time the line was to be built to the standard gauge, as the Great Western Railway was by this time committed to the conversion of all its lines to the standard gauge and

had already converted most of them.

The prospectuses issued by the Company in the years immediately preceding and following passage of the Act stressed the importance of the borough and district, and envisaged a considerable increase in traffic when the railway opened.

'Helston is the centre of an important and productive agricultural district. A large passenger, goods, mineral and fish traffic may be anticipated, while a railway will give the greatest impetus to the development of market gardening for which the district is so admirably adapted. The traffic between Helston and the towns and districts of Penzance and Marazion, Hayle, St Ives, Camborne and Redruth is already large and will doubtless much increase, with improved facilities of transit. An average return of at least £20 per mile per week may be expected.'

Traffic estimates were taken for 12 days prior to 14 November 1879 – 'so that no exceptional summer traffic be included' – and it was estimated that an annual income of £8,500 would be guaranteed.

'Negotiations have been entered into with the Great Western Railway Company, who are favourable to the line and the Directors have agreed to recommend the shareholders to work the line, when constructed, at fifty per cent of the gross receipts. These terms are considered very favourable and it is believed this would leave a good profit on the small amount of capital required.'

HELSTON RAILWAY COMPANY.

Incorporated by Special Act of Parliament.

UNDER WORKING AGREEMENT WITH THE
GREAT WESTERN RAILWAY.

CAPITAL £70,000, IN 3,500 SHARES OF £20 EACH.

BORROWING POWERS £23,000.

ISSUE of £59,660, being the BALANCE of the SHARE CAPITAL,

£10,340 HAVING BEEN LOCALLY SUBSCRIBED FOR.

Payable—£1 per Share on APPLICATION.
£4 ,, on ALLOTMENT.
£5 ,, on 1st JULY, 1882.
£5 ,, on 2nd OCTOBER, 1882.
£5 ,, on 1st JANUARY, 1883.
£20

Subscribers are at liberty to pay in advance all or any of the instalments, entitling them to receive interest at £5 per cent. per annum from the date of payment thereof.

The liability of Shareholders is limited to the amount of their Shares.

Interest at the rate of £5 per cent. per annum will be paid half-yearly upon the amount paid up in advance, as above, until the completion of the Line, and as a security for the due and punctual payment of the same the necessary sum will be invested in the names of two of the Directors of the Company.

The Contract for the construction of the Railway has been taken by a responsible contractor, and the Works are now being rapidly proceeded with.

The Great Western Railway have agreed to work and for ever repair and maintain the Line, free of all cost to the Helston Railway Company, for 50 per cent. of the gross receipts.

Directors.

WILLIAM BICKFORD-SMITH, Esq., J.P., Trevarno, near Helston (Chairman).
DAVID WISE BAIN, Esq., J.P., Messrs. Bain, Field, Hitchins & Co., Bankers, Redruth and Helston.
WILLIAM BOLITHO, Jun., Esq., J.P., Messrs. Bolitho, Sons & Co., Bankers, Helston and Penzance; Director of the Cornwall Railway.
RICHARD SKEWES MARTYN, Esq., J.P., Mayor of Helston.
RICHARD GUNDRY ROWS, Esq., Trisprison, near Helston.
W. MOLESWORTH-ST. AUBYN, Esq., M.P., 1, Brick Court, Temple, E.C.

Bankers.

THE CAPITAL & COUNTIES BANK, LIMITED, 39, Threadneedle Street, London, and Branches.
Messrs. BOLITHO, SONS & Co., Helston and Penzance.
Messrs. BAIN, FIELD, HITCHINS & Co., Helston and Redruth.

Engineers.

S. W. JENKIN, Esq., Liskeard, Cornwall.
R. E. WILSON, Esq., Delahay Street, Westminster.

Secretary & Solicitor.

J. R. DANIELL, Esq.

Offices.

CAMBORNE, CORNWALL.

PROSPECTUS.

THE Helston Railway Company has been incorporated by Special Act of Parliament, for the purpose of constructing a Railway from the Gwinear Road Station, on the main line of the Great Western and West Cornwall Railway, to the ancient Borough and Market Town of Helston, a distance of about 8¼ miles through an important agricultural and mineral district.

The construction of the Railway is in active progress, and it is anticipated that it will be open for traffic by June, 1883.

The shortest and cheapest route has been selected, and the one most likely to secure the greatest amount of traffic.

The proposed terminus at Helston has been chosen with a view to an extension of the Railway at a future date to the Lizard and to Porthleven and other adjacent districts, and at the same time to meet, as far as possible, the convenience of the town.

The traffic between Helston and the towns and district of Penzance and Marazion, Hayle, St. Ives, Camborne and Redruth, is already large and will doubtless much increase with improved facilities for transit.

Careful estimates of traffic based upon the actual number of persons entering and leaving Helston daily, and of the tonnage of goods traffic of the Borough and District, coupled with the experience on similar existing lines, give a revenue ample to admit of a good dividend on the invested capital.

These estimates of traffic are quite independent of that to and from Penryn, Falmouth, Truro, Porthleven, and the South of Helston, much of which will of necessity pass over the Railway when constructed.

A map of West Cornwall, in which the proposed Line is delineated in red and existing Lines are shown in black, accompanies this Prospectus, and a reference to it will show a very large and fertile agricultural district, of which Helston occupies a central position, and is the only Market Town.

The District, besides its extensive area, possesses the following special advantages:—

A great portion of the land lying South of Helston, is well adapted for Market Gardening, and only the want of proper means of transit has hitherto prevented large quantities of garden produce from being rendered available for the Markets, and populous towns of the Kingdom. Connection with the Great Western Line will open up an Industry in this direction, capable of very great expansion.

The Fishing Stations in the Meneage District, which are most advantageously situated, have hitherto remained without enterprise, owing to the difficulties in sending the fish to distant Markets; and it is confidently believed, that with the means of conveyance the present undertaking will provide, the Fishing Trade of the District will receive such an impetus, as will at no

The Coast scenery of Meneage, including Mullion, Kynance and the Lizard, is almost universally acknowledged to stand alone in its endless variety and beauty. The tediousness of reaching it by coach has, up to this time, prevented great numbers of persons from becoming acquainted with it, and it is not too much to say that with the projected Railway communication, several of the Coves of the District will be among the most popular places of summer resort in the Kingdom.

The want of railway communication between Helston and district, and the main trunk system of the Great Western Railway, has been urgently felt for many years, and the undertaking has so well commended itself to the traders and others in Helston than the sum of £10,340 has already been subscribed by them towards the construction of the Railway.

The Great Western Railway, recognising the importance of the Line, have entered into an agreement to work and for ever maintain and repair the same, free of all cost to the Helston Railway Company, for 50 per cent. of the gross receipts.

The practical effect of this Agreement is such that the Helston Railway Company will have one entire half of the gross receipts from tolls and fares for division amongst its Shareholders, the whole of the outgoings and expenses connected with the Railway, except the small Establishment charges, being defrayed by the Great Western Company.

The Directors are convinced that the estimates based on existing circumstances alone, are quite sufficient to justify the expectation of a fair dividend on the capital invested; but when the development of the neighbourhood by the extension of the Market Gardening and Fishing Industries, which the Line will occasion, is also considered, it is evident that the Helston Railway must speedily become a very valuable property.

Prospectuses and Forms of Application can be obtained of either of the Bankers of the Company, or of the Secretary and Solicitor, John R. Daniell, Esq., Camborne, Cornwall, by any of whom Applications for Shares in the form herewith will be received.

April, 1882.

It was estimated that the cost of the standard gauge line would be £70,000 inclusive of the cost of the land required, and the Act allowed for the issue of £70,000 worth of stock with borrowing powers for a further £23,333. Further issues of stock of £6,000 were respectively authorised by the Great Western Railway (No 1) Act of 1882 (45 & 46 Vic c214) ('the 1882 Act')

and the Great Western Railway Act 1885 (48 & 49 Vic c147) ('the 1885 Act').

Section 29 of the Act provided that the Company's powers of compulsory purchase would cease after three years and, perhaps even more importantly, section 36 stated that if the railway was not completed within five years from the passing of the Act then 'the powers

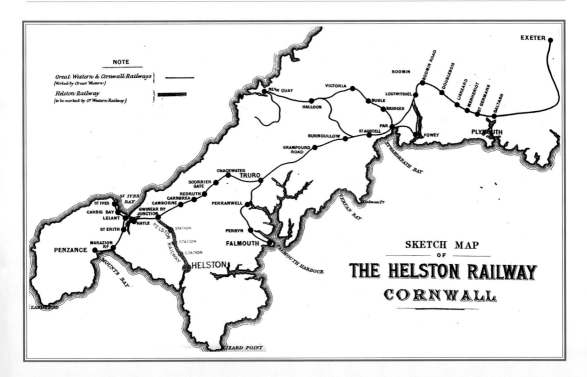

for making and completing the Railways or otherwise in relation thereto shall cease to be exercised except as to so much thereof as is then completed'.

By an agreement reached on 5 April 1882, the GWR agreed inter alia to construct the works at Gwinear Road and to give the Helston Railway free use thereof for seven years. The GWR also agreed to maintain the permanent way and track after the initial period of 12 months, and covenanted to provide the staff (except the Secretary and his staff), locomotive power and rolling stock. After the opening, any capital advanced by the GWR was to be a debt due at 5% interest, and receipts less passenger duty were to be divided 50:50. Clause 29 of the agreement provided that it should be in perpetuity, and clause 31 stated that, under the provisions of the Railway Companies Arbitration Act 1859, any dispute should be settled by the leading QC of the Northern Circuit.

In 1884/85 the directors arranged with the GWR that a rebate of 5% would be allowed on all traffic over its system that originated from, or had its destination upon, the Helston line. The 1885 Act empowered the Company to cancel £56,000 of ordinary stock and to convert a similar amount of share capital into 3.5% preference stock, the latter to rank pari passu with the ordinary stock after the payment of their dividend.

Practical work on the construction of the line began on Wednesday 22 March 1882. Amidst great rejoicing in the town, the first sod was cut by the Mayor, R. S. Martyn Esq, JP. The ceremony took place in the Tile House

Field, near the site of the proposed station, whither a large procession had wound its way through triumphal arches from the Bowling Green at the bottom of the town. Ceremonial arches were erected in Coinagehall Street, Church Street (near the Corn Exchange and near Cross Street), Meneage Street and Wendron Street, and in Coinagehall Street fir trees were planted alternating with Venetian masts. The messages on the ceremonial arches were enthusiastic and optimistic. The grandest arch in Coinagehall Street included 'Success to the Helston Railway; One and All; Union is Strength; Prosperity to the Trade of Helston; Fish, Tin and Copper', while one in Church Street proclaimed 'May Trade Increase' and 'Progression'. The procession was made up of the Helston Volunteer Band, the Oddfellows, the Rational Society, Freemasons, the Truro Volunteer Band, Railway Directors and Officials, Borough dignitaries and Shareholders. In the afternoon a free tea was given to the children and aged persons of the town, and the day was concluded by a display of fireworks at 8.00pm. The centrepiece of the display was a 'Special Device' – 'Success to the Helston Railway' – surrounded by a fringe of golden fire.

Details of the celebrations were recorded by a William Roskilly of Coverack in a letter to Edwin Richards of London dated 28 April 1882, a copy of which was kindly been supplied to me by his great-grandson. His letter runs to more than seven pages (in typed format), but his contemporaneous comments are of such interest that some extracts should be reproduced connection with the Sunday Schools, the eagerness being the more intent on account of the preceding days being rather unpleasant by wind and rain.'

In the event, all was well...

'...with a north-westerly wind and with two showers of rain during the early part of the morning all that we had unpleasant, much to the joy of all Helston.
'From the hours of 8.00am to 12 Noon, omnibuses, carriages, waggonettes, phaetons, bicycles, tricycles and want not were pouring into the town, one after another and all together, and in addition to these, a great number of pedestrians were seen wending their way towards the peaceful Borough.
'At the Tile House Field, there was a grandstand erected which seated about 200 people, and the field was crowded as well.'

As was the custom at the time, the celebrations included a banquet. After the procession had wound its way back to the centre of the town,

'...the Mayor, Directors, Corporation with many other gentlemen entered the Angel Hotel where a grand dinner was awaiting them, after which for a dessert they partook of speeches, which report

Invitation to 'Cutting the first Turf', 22 March 1882. *Public Record Office*

here.
William Roskilly states that it had been intended that the date for the cutting of the first sod had originally been fixed for Wednesday 8 March 1882, but that 'owing to some unseen and unknown circumstance [sic]' it was delayed until 22 March. He was particularly impressed by the arrangements for the celebrations on the day.
Once the town had decided

'...to begin the thing well, public meetings were held in the Guildhall, which were ably presided over by the Mayor, who is a commercial star, to form committees to carry out the day's proceedings successfully. First and foremost the money was to be collected, for as the old saying goes – "Money makes the mare to go". A public meeting was then held to appoint committees formed of the businessmen of the town to look after the decorations, to superintend the free tea and see that the fireworks were carried successfully.
'The morn of 22 March was eagerly watched by the inhabitants, an eagerness which is rivalled in the Borough only on Flora Day or on the Tea Drinking Festivals in

The Toast List at the luncheon commemorating the cutting of the first sod. *Helston Museum*

Poster advertising the ceremony of the cutting of the first sod. *Helston Museum*

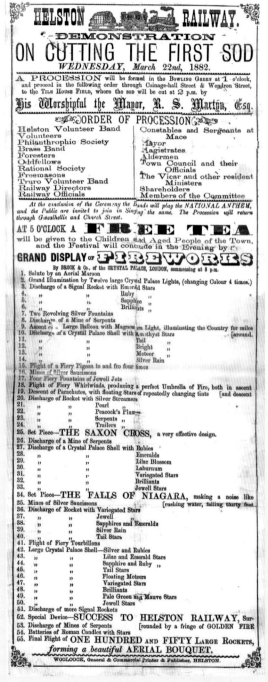

Programme for the celebrations taking place on the same day. *Helston Museum*

says were of a very pleasing character.'

Not long after the initial ceremony, section 20 of the 1882 Act authorised two short extensions to the planned line. Section 20 (1) permitted a short extension (2 furlongs and 3.20 chains in length) over the level crossing into Gwinear Road station, while Section 20 (2) authorised an extension 5 furlongs and 9 chains in length from the originally authorised end of the line at Helston (adjacent to Godolphin Road) to a point 33 yards south of the town prison (i.e. at the top of and to the rear of Wendron Street and near the junction of Sanctuary Lane and Parc an Dower). The new station was to be approached by a roadway about 300 yards from the top of Wendron Street. This extension to the town centre, which required a bridge of at least 15 feet in height over the former turnpike road (now Godolphin Road), was never constructed because it proved impossible to raise the additional £3,000 capital required.

For the following six months the work was prosecuted with some activity by Mr E. D. Maddison, the contractor who had agreed to do the work at the Engineer's prices and to take a considerable number of

Of the ceremonial arches erected in the town to mark the ceremony of the cutting of the first sod, that in the principal thoroughfare – Coinagehall Street – was the grandest and largest, incorporated no fewer than two arches for vehicular traffic and two smaller arches for pedestrians. Its message reads 'SUCCESS TO THE HELSTON RAILWAY' and also refers on the left arch to the industries upon which Helston and the surrounding area depended at the time – 'FISH, TIN AND COPPER'. The right-hand arch bears the motto of Cornwall, 'ONE AND ALL'. The construction was clearly of some strength, as it is bearing the weight of seven sturdy citizens.

The second photograph is taken from further away, and shows not only the arches but also the trees planted for the occasion and the alternate Venetian masts referred to in the local newspaper. This photograph shows the 'beautiful curve' of the street, which the late Sir John Betjeman likened to The High in Oxford. *Original 1882 photographs on card from author's collection*

Two ceremonial arches were erected in Church Street. The message on that at the junction with Cross Street is hard to distinguish, but appears to read 'PERSEVERANCE ENSURES SUCCESS', but the message 'MAY TRADE INCREASE' cannot be missed on the arch supported (on the right) by the Corn Exchange near the junction with Coinagehall Street. In the background to the arch near Cross Street can be seen the entrance to and part of St. Michael's Church, which was rebuilt by the Earl of Godolphin after an earlier church had been damaged when the tower was struck by lightning in 1727. With the exception of an out-of-scale Post Office built in 1961 on the left and immediately adjacent to the arch in Coinagehall Street, almost all the buildings in Coinagehall Street and Church Street remain substantially unchanged in 2012. *Original 1882 photographs on card from author's collection*

Above: A simpler structure was constructed in Meneage Street proclaiming 'RAILWAY AND INCREASE IN TRADE'. Here again the buildings are little changed, although the chapel to the right has been converted into flats after a period in use as squash courts. *Helston Museum*

Below: Crowds surround the Directors of the Company and the Mayor of Helston – R. S. Martyn – and other distinguished guests as the Mayor prepares to cut the first sod of turf in the Tile House Field. The silver engraved spade and the ceremonial wheelbarrow are preserved in the Helston Museum (see page 127). *Original 1882 photograph on card from author's collection*

The major engineering work on the line was the construction of the viaduct over the Cober valley near the village of Lowertown, a mile from Helston. The structure is officially known as the Cober Viaduct, but is generally referred to as the Lowertown Viaduct. Martin Matthews, a former curator of Helston Museum and a Bard of Cornwall with the Cornish name of Carer Hellys (Lover of Helston), managed to acquire some photographs of the branch under construction, including a number of the viaduct, which I believe have not been published before. These show the wooden centring in place for four arches and work in progress on the fifth; one granite arch (far right, nearest to Helston) has been completed. *Both Martin Matthews collection*

shares in the Company. However, it soon became clear that Mr Maddison could not fulfil his engagement and at the beginning of 1884 the work was suspended. Given that the Company's powers to build the line were due to expire in the following year, this must have caused considerable alarm to the Directors, but the situation was redeemed by section 42 of the 1885 Act, which extended the powers for the construction of the railway by another three years until 9 July 1888. It was not until the middle of 1886 that the Directors could report that new contractors had agreed to carry out the contract and were proceeding with the 'greatest energy and in a most satisfactory manner'. The new contractors were Messrs Lang & Son of Liskeard, who had completed Angarrack Viaduct on the main line to the west of Gwinear Road in the previous year (opened 4 October 1885).

By the middle of 1886 the Engineer's report stated that all the cuttings had been completed and only the slopes of the cuttings near the Cober Viaduct and the formations at Gwinear Road and Helston remained to be finished. The Cober Viaduct itself and all the bridges were practically complete and the track, being laid at three-quarters of a mile per week, was laid over 5½ miles. The station buildings were not yet fully erected but by the beginning of 1887 those at Praze were finished except for the furnishings. At Nancegollan the signal box was fixed and at Helston the platform and goods shed had been put up and the passenger buildings and signal box were almost finished. The sidings were being laid

there, and only at Gwinear Road had much still to be done.

By October 1886 works had progressed sufficiently to enable the directors to travel over the line in a contractor's wagon provided by Mr Lang.

All was ready by the beginning of May 1887, and the railway was inspected by the Inspector of the Board of Trade – Colonel Rich RE – on Friday 6 May 1887. The *Cornish Telegraph* of 12 May reported that, after being met at Gwinear Road, Colonel Rich

'...took his station on the locomotive, to which was attached a brake van and a passenger coach. He made a minute examination of the different viaducts and other points of interest on the line, and expressed himself as highly pleased with the construction of the entire system.'

Afterwards, he was entertained to a private lunch at Helston station and intimated his intention of granting a certificate for the opening of the line forthwith.

A correspondent in the *West Briton* reported that Colonel Rich returned to London on the 5 o'clock mail train from Penzance, which 'made a special stoppage at Gwinear Road' station to pick him up, together with officials of the GWR. The GWR was immediately informed of the result of Colonel Rich's inspection and indicated that the line could be formally opened on the following Monday.

At very short notice, therefore, the line was

The quality of the construction and the grandeur of the viaduct justify these two photographs of the finished work, pristine and probably as yet not crossed by a train. More than 125 years later, the viaduct continues to span the valley as good as new. *Both Martin Matthews collection*

The pristine state of the ballast, track and buildings and the absence of any railway vehicles indicate that these two photographs of Helston station were taken shortly before the line opened for traffic on 9 May 1887. The station building and the engine shed are sturdily built and fully justify the statement by the Board of Trade's inspector, Colonel Rich RE, that he was 'highly pleased with the construction of the entire system'. The station building was about 100 feet in length and was not dissimilar to that constructed at St Ives in 1877, although the latter was built on a curve. Perhaps because it would have been demolished in the event of the construction of the proposed extension to the centre of Helston. The carriage shed seen in the far distance – the most southerly piece of track in Great Britain – was made of wood and survived only until the 1950s. *Both Martin Matthews collection*

After some many years of heartache and expense, the opening day finally dawned on Monday 9 May 1887. The Mayor, Directors and other dignitaries assembled in front of the new station building, not far from the spot where the first sod had been cut five years previously. Given the short notice between the approval of the line by Colonel Rich on Friday 6 May and the opening day, it must have taken some organisation to arrange the attendance of so many VIPs, but few would have wished to miss this important episode in local history or the customary repast at the Angel afterwards. By arranging such a speedy opening of the line, the Directors were able to provide services on the following day for visitors to Flora Day. *Helston Museum*

opened for traffic on Monday 9 May, the day before Flora Day, and the local paper commended the fact that the arrangements were 'considering this fact, very satisfactory'. The trains were worked from the start by the GWR. The first train, decorated with evergreens and flags, started from Helston at 9.40am and conveyed about 50 passengers free of charge to Gwinear Road. A 'well-filled' train returned at 10.37am, but the Directors did not return until 12.50pm. At Praze they were presented with an address by the Rev J.W. Johns, Vicar of Crowan, on behalf of himself and his parishioners:

'As Vicar of Crowan for more than 40 years, I beg on behalf of the churchwardens, the parishioners, and myself to join in the congratulations which are being offered this day to the directors on the opening of the Helston branch of the West Cornwall Railway [sic]. We have been anxiously expecting this important event; and as more than a third of the new railway passes through the parish of Crowan, we naturally take a deep interest in its welfare. We will not detain you further than to offer our sincere congratulations, and to wish you Godspeed in the best and truest sense of the expression.'

William Bickford-Smith returned thanks on behalf of the Directors. By 1887 he had formally adopted by deed poll the double-barrelled surname that he had been using since 1868, and had been elected in 1885 as the MP for the local constituency. There were no speeches at Nancegollan, although a few passengers joined the train there.

Meanwhile, in Helston, the Mayor and Corporation, accompanied by the band of the Rifle Volunteers, processed to the station at 1.00pm and found the station decorated with bunting and 'presenting a pretty appearance'. At 1.20pm the Directors' train entered the station amidst applause, the sound of fog signals and the playing by the band of 'See the Conquering Hero Comes'. This Handelian piece was particularly popular with Victorians on occasions such as this. Prayers specially composed for the occasion were offered by the Rev Canon Tyack, and the Mayor read an address of congratulations:

'To the Directors of the Helston Railway, and the Contractor, the engineer and their staff, and to the official representatives of the Great Western Company.

'Gentlemen, on the opening of the Helston Railway, we, the Mayor, Aldermen and Councillors and the inhabitants of the Borough of Helston, and the neighbourhood, beg to offer you, and to all who have been employed in the undertaking, our hearty

Given that the construction of the line had been well recorded in photographs, it is perhaps surprising that only one photograph of the first train is known to exist. It is believed to show the 9.40am service to Gwinear Road, made up of six carriages and a brake-van, standing in Helston station. There appears to be one open wagon in the goods shed. *Helston Museum*

congratulations, and to welcome your presence on this auspicious occasion with the greatest pleasure. We have watched with much interest the progress of the railway and are very sensible of the difficulties with which you have had to contend in its construction. The completion of this work, so long desired, cannot fail to promote the interests and development of the towns and neighbourhood, and to induce a satisfactory result to the directors and shareholders generally. You will pardon the shortness of our address, which is intended, at least, to convey to you our sentiment of admiration at the amount of energy and perseverance displayed in effecting the completion of the works, and our most sincere and best wishes for the success of the Helston Railway. Given under the corporate seal this ninth day of May 1887.'

The address was signed by the Mayor, Mr F.V. Hill, and countersigned by Mr J. G. Plomer (Town Clerk).

The guard on the first train was George Sainthill Lindsey, who continued in the post of guard until his retirement in 1921. When interviewed on his 90th birthday in 1937, he mentioned that he had offered his services as guard again in 1926 during the General Strike and had carried out the duties on the restricted service that ran for one week.

Again Mr Bickford-Smith responded, stressing how thankful the Directors were to arrive at this day after more than five years of arduous, tiresome and wearisome labour.

The Directors, members of the Corporation, the band, corporate officials and friends (including my great-great-grandfather) then proceeded to Gwinear Road, returning at 3.10pm for a luncheon, numerous speeches and toasts in the Angel Hotel, presided over by the Mayor.

Immediately after the opening, the *West Briton* recorded:

'Yet another link was added to the great railway chain of the country on Monday last, when the branch railway Gwinear Road to Helston was opened to traffic. In these days of unprecedented enterprise and progress it can hardly be imagined that such an important district as that which surrounds Helston has up to the present possessed no direct railway service. Such, however, is the case and but for the noble efforts of a few local gentlemen the want would not now have been supplied.'

Traffic during the first few months was considered most satisfactory, but there was some falling off during the winter. The receipts for the period between July and December 1888 (£1,617 18s 2d) showed a slight improvement over the corresponding period in 1887 (£1,515 12s 8d). Traffic in 1889

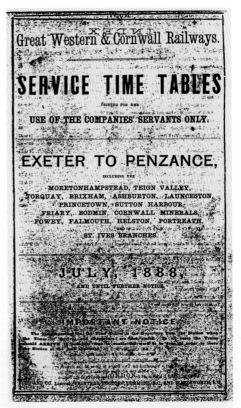

The Helston Branch timetable from the 'Great Western & Cornwall Railways Service Time Tables printed for the use of the companies' servants only ... July 1888 and until further notice'. *Author's collection*

HELSTON BRANCH

Distance	STATIONS	Passenger arr.	Passenger dep.	Mixed, Pass. and Goods arr.	Mixed, Pass. and Goods dep.	Passenger arr.	Passenger dep.	Passenger arr.	Passenger dep.	Passenger arr.	Passenger dep.	Passenger arr.	Passenger dep.	Distance	STATIONS	Passenger arr.	Passenger dep.	Mixed, Pass. and Goods arr.	Mixed, Pass. and Goods dep.	Passenger arr.	Passenger dep.	Passenger arr.	Passenger dep.	Passenger arr.	Passenger dep.	Pass. arr.	Pass. dep.
		A.M.	A.M.	A.M.	A.M.	P.M.	P.M.			P.M.	P.M.	P.M.	P.M.			A.M.	A.M.			P.M.	P.M.	P.M.	P.M.	P.M.	P.M.	P.M.	P.M.
	Helston	....	9 40	...	11 35	...	1 48	....	4 35	....	6 40	....	7 48		Gwinear Rd.	...	10 37	...	12 50	...	2 45	...	6 7	...	7 15	....	8 38
4	Nancegollan	9 50	9 51	11 45	11 48	1 58	1 59	4 45	4 46	6 50	6 51	7 58	7 59		Praze	10 44	10 46	12 57	1 1	2 52	2 53	6 14	6 15	7 22	7 23	8 45	8 46
6	Prnze	9 56	9 57	11 53	11 55	2 4	2 5	4 51	4 52	6 56	6 57	8 4	8 5		Nancegollan	10 50	10 51	1 6	1 10	2 58	2 59	6 20	6 21	7 28	7 29	8 51	8 52
9	Gwinear Rd.	10 5	....	12 5	....	2 13	....	5 0	....	7 5	....	8 13	....		Helston	11 2	....	1 21	....	3 10	....	6 32	....	7 40	....	9 3	....

NO SUNDAY TRAINS. The Helston Line is a Narrow Gauge Single Line, worked by Train Staff. The Train Staff is a round one, painted black, and lettered "Gwinear Road and Helston." Only One Engine in Steam must be allowed to be on this Branch at one and the same time. Until Further Notice the Block Telegraph between Helston and Gwinear Road will **NOT** be worked.

The Last Train Helston — Flora Day

Until the growth of bus and car travel, the branch probably carried more passengers on Flora Day than on any other day in the year, although the crush is unlikely to have been as bad as that envisaged by Cynicus, the artist in this postcard of 'The Last Train – Helston Flora Day'. *Helston Museum*

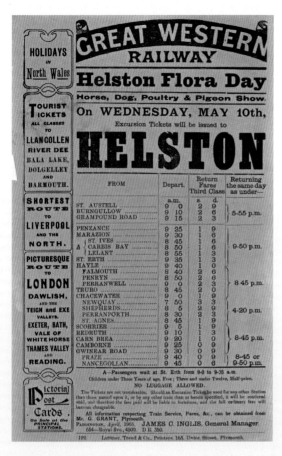

GWR Helston Flora Day Excursion Ticket leaflet, 1905.
Author's collection

(between Praze and Nancegollan). The train crew and the single passenger passed the night in the train and reached a nearby farm next morning. Work commenced on clearing the line on the Thursday, and 200 men managed to finish the work by Saturday 14th. The men were then sent by train to Helston, which had in the meantime been completely cut off from the outside world, where they were 'received with cheers by the townspeople who had congregated on the platform'.

The maintenance of the permanent way was taken over by the GWR on 9 May 1888, after which some of the curves were improved and double flanging completed. The use of Gwinear Road without payment ended in May 1894, but agreement was reached as to its continued use at £50 per annum. Soon, however, the Directors proposed to the GWR that it should purchase the line, and a price of £7 for each £20 share was agreed. Amalgamation was completed on 1 July 1898 and the line was vested in the GWR by section 61 of the Great Western Railway (General Powers) Act 1898 (61 & 62 Vic c174), which received Royal Assent on 2 August 1898.

No doubt in preparation for the takeover, the GWR carried out an exercise that would now be called 'due diligence'. This revealed the fact that parts of the route of the line had not actually been legally conveyed to the Company, and the deeds indicate that the freehold title to parts of the line was not legally transferred until 1898! Meanwhile, the Company was responsible for, and perhaps did not always promptly pay, rent, as demonstrated by it being named as the Defendant in a County Court demand in February 1894 issued by John Peverell Rogers and Reginald Nankivell Rogers. The sum claimed was £2 1s 0d, including six years' rent! Two months later, judgement was given for the additional sum of 15s 6d for costs incurred by the plaintiffs in preparing a subpoena for a witness.

Although this sum may seem trivial today, it was not an insubstantial sum in the 1890s, and clearly exercised the parties' respective solicitors. The plaintiffs' solicitors sought to avoid litigation by giving notice of intended court proceedings:

'I beg to inform you that as my forbearance only seems to be a pretext for further delay and inaction on the part of the Company, my client has instructed me on the first available day after the opening of the Courts after the long vacation to apply for a mandamus without delay...'

...while elsewhere reference is made to the failure to respond to letters as 'very unbusinesslike'.

The debt was ultimately paid and the plaintiffs' solicitor sought his costs, albeit in a gentlemanly way: 'Your firm has given me enough trouble in this little matter to charge double what I have, besides putting me in a scrape with my client who brooks no delay, but you are personally such a good 'un...' that no addition fees were demanded!

was further increased as the result of the Royal Cornwall Agriculture Society's Exhibition being held in the town, whilst in 1890 this was maintained to some extent by improved connections with the down 'Cornishman' train. In 1891 the Directors were pleased to note that the GWR system was being converted to standard gauge as rapidly as possible and the anticipated increase in traffic that it was hoped would accompany the conversion first became noticeable at the end of 1892.

It is interesting to note in connection with the conversion of the broad gauge in May 1892 that on Saturday 21 May a special service was run on the Helston branch because some of the stock was required elsewhere. One Tricomposite and two Thirds were 'borrowed' for the St Ives line on Monday 23 May, and left the Helston line very depleted in stock.

In the previous year, the branch had been completely blocked by snow for almost a week during the Great Blizzard of March 1891. On the evening of Tuesday 10 March an evening train from Gwinear Road ran into a 15-foot drift in the half-mile-long Polcrebo Farm cutting

Before taking part in the Mid-Day Furry Dance on 8 May 1907, Sir William Treloar, Lord Mayor of London, received the freedom of the Borough of Helston in the Guildhall before processing down Coinagehall Street to a more informal ceremony at the foot of the Grylls Monument. Here, under a banner bearing the legend 'Helston children unite with the Lord Mayor in helping crippled children', Sir William received a cheque for £50 (a considerable sum, being roughly the annual income of an agricultural labourer at the time) towards his target of £60,000 (maybe £4 million today) in his 'great scheme' to erect homes for crippled children. In addition he received a further 7s 6d raised by children of the Helston branch of the Waifs and Strays Society. The Treloar Trust continues in 2012 and operates the Treloar's College for Physically Disabled Students at Alton, Hampshire, providing education, care, therapy, medical support and independence in preparation for adult life.

After the takeover by the GWR, the line settled down to a quiet existence, providing a service to the local community with little fuss or bother. In 1907 it carried what may have been its most distinguished passenger when the Lord Mayor of London, Sir William Treloar, arrived on 7 May in a special saloon attached to the normal service, which arrived punctually in bright sunshine at 5.15pm. He was received 'with hearty cheers' at the station, decorated with flags and a portion of the platform laid with carpet, and the *Western Morning News* (*WMN*) reported that my great-great-grandfather was among those receiving him at the station. The Lord Mayor then proceeded to the centre of the town under banners proclaiming 'Welcome to the Lord Mayor and Sheriffs'. Sir William's family had close links with Helston, and he arranged his visit during his year as Lord Mayor to receive the freedom of the borough and to take part in the Furry Dance on the following day.

On Flora Day itself, according to a report in the *WMN*, the GWR provided no fewer than 26 trains to Helston instead of the usual eight services. 'A large number of extra railway officials were on duty, and the arrangements for the arrival and despatch of trains worked most smoothly and efficiently,' it reported.

During the General Strike in 1926, which commenced on Tuesday 4 May and was settled on 14 May, no trains ran on the branch at the outset, but services to/from Helston recommenced on Monday the 10th. As a consequence of his activities during the strike, the Station Master at Nancegollan was transferred to another position. Another consequence of the General Strike was a temporary reduction in services on the branch due to a shortage of coal, as a result of which the GWR introduced a temporary bus service to and from Camborne. This became permanent in November and no doubt extracted some custom from the railway.

It has been suggested that the Helston branch was occasionally patrolled during the Second World War by an armoured train hauled by an ex-Great Eastern Railway Class 'F4' 2-4-2T locomotive. This train certainly operated in Cornwall, but I have not been able to verify if it ever came to Helston.

The Helston branch was 8 miles 69 chains in length and was single track throughout. A passing loop was provided between 1908 and 1937 at Nancegollan Crossing Place (south of Polcrebo Farm, between Praze and Nancegollan), and from 1937 in Nancegollan station itself. Until the opening of the crossing loop, the line was worked on the basis of 'one engine in steam', but after the intermediate box was opened in 1908 the Electric Train staff system was used. The line cost £100,000 to build, of which £9,000 was spent on the acquisition of land and £6,000 on the construction of the Cober Viaduct.

The branch left the main line of the former West Cornwall Railway at Gwinear Road, 316 miles from Paddington via Bristol, or 294½ miles from Paddington via the 20th-century cut-off route, and 2½ miles west of Camborne. The *Western Daily Mercury* reported at the opening that 'a fine station has been built at Gwinear Road: the unpretentious stopping place of a year ago has disappeared and periodic travellers are surprised at the transformation affected'. Leaving Gwinear Road, the branch headed eastwards from the island platform adjoining the down main line and crossed the level crossing parallel with but independent of the main line, then climbed for half a mile at 1 in 60 through a deepish cutting. After a curve to the south, this was followed by a little over a mile of almost level track where the highest speeds of the journey were usually recorded. The late Peter Semmens, whose articles on train timings in *The Railway Magazine* were legendary, timed two branch trains on this section on 7 August 1951 and recorded speeds up to 41mph southbound behind No 4545 and more than 44mph on the return journey behind No 4566.

The climb recommenced three-quarters of a mile before Praze (2¾ miles), the first station on the line and situated conveniently for the village with the unusual name of Praze-an-Beeble. This single platform and one siding, originally a goods-only loop, for many years gave the impression of being little used, as was also the large water tower completed in 1888 and situated at the north end of the station. The station name board (which only announced 'Praze') was unusual for the branch in that it was made of blue vitreous enamel while, in later years at least, all the other stations sported standard GWR-type chocolate and cream running-in boards. About 25 chains before Praze, the line crossed the Penzance-Redruth road (now the B3280) by the Bold Gate Bridge, then immediately before the station itself it crossed the road between Camborne and Helston (now the B3303). These were the only main-road bridges on the branch that were not built with granite arches, but were metal girder structures on granite supports.

After a few yards of level track through the station, the line climbed for a mile at 1 in 62, 1 in 185 and 1 in 265 to the summit near Crowan. From here the line fell to Nancegollan (5¼ miles), passing at milepost 4¾ the site of the passing loop that opened after the

works had been inspected by H. A. Yorke of the Railway Department of the Board of Trade. In his report dated 2 January 1909 he recorded that 'the new works comprise the construction of a passing loop and the provision of a new signal box, together with the necessary signals. The signal box contains 8 levers and 5 spare levers. Safety catch points have been provided at the south end of the new up loop line.' The loop and signal box were removed in September 1937 when Nancegollan was rebuilt. Nancegollan Crossing Signal Box had previously seen service at St Germans Viaduct, from which site it was moved on completion of the new section of the Cornish main line between Wearde (west of Saltash) and St Germans when a double-track inland deviation was opened to avoid the expense of reconstructing a number of Brunel's wooden single-line viaducts over creeks of the River Tamar. In 1937 a second platform, a passing loop and new station buildings were provided at Nancegollan, and siding accommodation was further increased to meet Admiralty needs in 1945. Nancegollan was the largest intermediate station on the line and, especially on summer Saturdays, some branch trains used to cross here before the passenger services were withdrawn. A camping coach was located here between 1958 and 1962, but at no other time. Originally the maximum speed permitted between Gwinear Road and Nancegollan was 35mph, and 25mph thence to a point about 30 chains outside Helston, even though Peter Semmens's records demonstrate that these limits were not always observed. In 1951 he recorded speeds of up to 39mph south of Nancegollan. On the final approach to Helston, speed should not exceed 15mph.

Beyond Nancegollan the line curved away to the left, undulating and curving over the next 2 miles to Truthall Halt (7 miles), opened by the GWR in July 1905, probably on the 3rd when a railmotor service was introduced. However, it is interesting to note that a station in the approximate location of Truthall Halt features on the map accompanying the original prospectus. The station name board on this typical GWR halt, graced with a typical GWR 'pagoda' shelter, proclaimed it to be indeed Truthall Halt, but tickets bought at Helston during the last three years of the passenger service called it either Truthall Platform or Truthall Bridge Halt. Its name was changed to Truthall Platform in the timetable in July 1906. It was closed completely from 5 November 1962.

The halt was built near the top of a bank of 1 in 60 and 1 in 77 that dropped down to the rock cuttings that preceded the largest and most expensive structure on the line – the Cober Viaduct. This was known locally as the Lowertown Viaduct, after the village over which it still gently curves. It is built of local granite hewn from beside the railway; is more than 100 yards long, is 90 feet above the valley floor at its highest point, and comprises six spans each of 50 feet. In order to minimise the engineering work required, the line dropped steeply down one side of the valley parallel with the river before completing a horse-shoe turn to face southwards to

Helston along the other side of the valley. Beyond the viaduct, the line climbed again at 1 in 60 through another rock cutting before dropping over the last mile into the cutting and bridge that marked the approach to the level of Helston station.

Helston, although the terminus of the line, boasted only a single platform on the right-hand side of the track. Beyond, the line continued for about 200 yards on an embankment as far as Godolphin Road to the site of a carriage shed, removed in about 1958. At the Gwinear Road end of the station, a signal box stood beside the entrance to a single-road engine shed, while a goods shed spanned one of the run-round sidings. A licensed and privately operated refreshment room offered a service rare at such a small branch terminus, and for many years served as the local pub for this part of the town. The refreshment room closed after the departure of the last passenger train on 3 November 1962. The station was situated almost a mile north of the centre of the town although, as mentioned earlier, parliamentary powers were obtained but never invoked to extend the line to a more central location. The station's somewhat inconvenient location was justified in the prospectuses of the Company:

'The proposed terminus at Helston has been chosen with a view to an extension of the Railway, at a future date, to the Lizard and other adjacent districts and at the same time to meet, as far as possible, the convenience of the town.'

A ticket platform at Helston was closed on 1 January 1903, after which date tickets were collected at Nancegollan.

An extension to the Lizard was in fact planned at the turn of the century, and a Light Railway Order (LRO) was sought by local promoters – Archibald Scott, Pearce Jenkin and Samuel Mott – under the provisions of the Light Railways Act 1896. Following a public inquiry held in Helston on 21 October 1897, the Light Railway Commissioners under the chairmanship of the Earl of Jersey GCMG made the Lizard Light Railway Order 1898. This was confirmed by the Board of Trade on 21 April 1898, and Extension of Time and Amendment Orders were granted in 1901 and 1902 respectively.

The LRO authorised the construction by the Lizard Light Railway Company of a standard gauge railway 11 miles and 2 furlongs in length to be worked by 'steam or such other motive power as the Board of Trade may approve'. Although the Order required at least three fixed stations to be provided, it then went on to specify four – one near Dodson's Gap (2 miles 3 furlongs from Helston), one near Trevassack (5 miles), one near Penhale (7 miles 4½ furlongs), and one at the terminus at The Lizard. Five roads were required to be taken over the railway, and six single-span bridges over roads were specified, including one over Godolphin Road in Helston (immediately beyond the boundary with the existing

railway) with a span of 30 feet. Being a light railway, a maximum speed of 25mph was imposed.

One of the engineers employed by the promoters was Sir James Szlumper, who estimated that the cost of the line would be £61,587. Sir James's son and grandson both went on to become in turn Chief Engineers of the Southern Railway. The grandson, G. S. Szlumper, was even appointed General Manager of the Southern Railway in 1937.

It would appear from correspondence with the GWR that the promoters had given assurances to the Light Railway Commissioners that there would be no difficulty in raising the capital for the railway, but that once the Order had been obtained they had looked to the GWR to finance the undertaking. This the GWR declined to do, having concluded that 'the traffic of the District to be served would be insufficient (in any case for some time to come) to render a line remunerative.' Indeed, even in 1899 the GWR was expressing the view that it already had 'far too many unproductive lines upon our system to justify us in adding to their number'.

Despite the Extension of Time orders, the finance was not forthcoming and the line was not built. However, as an alternative, the GWR decided to experiment with an innovative motor bus service.

On 13 August 1903 the Chairman of the GWR announced at a General Meeting of shareholders that the Board had growing doubts about the justification for a number of light railways under consideration and that it was considering introducing feeders to its railway system by means of 'motor cars'. He continued:

'We have therefore given instruction for the purchase of five motors which will each carry 22 passengers. They will be petrol motors. They will go, not at 50mph speed, but I hope at a moderate speed. We shall be able to give convenience to the public in places where it is wanted, and we shall then be in a position to find out what traffic there is in the district. When we find that out we shall be in a position to determine whether it is a place suitable for a Light railway and whether there is any traffic that will pay. The first car will run from Helston to The Lizard.'

The consideration of this experiment by the GWR must have been well advanced by the time of the Chairman's statement, because the experimental service was introduced only four days later on 17 August 1903. Although the service was interrupted for a short period between September 1904 and April 1905 – the local authority refused to repair the road, and two buses had been destroyed by fire – the success of the bus service was demonstrated not only by the subsequent decision by the GWR not to build the light railway but also by the fact that a regular bus service between Helston and The Lizard survives to this day. A second service from Helston station was introduced to Porthleven in 1908, by which time numerous other bus services had been introduced by the GWR throughout its system. All

GWR bus services in Devon and Cornwall were taken over by the Western National Omnibus Company, in which the GWR held a 50% stake, at the end of 1928.

On 17 August 1953 a tablet was unveiled on the station wall by senior British Railways (Western Region) officers recording the 50th anniversary of this ground-breaking experiment. As had happened after ceremonies in 1882 and 1887, this ceremony was followed by the customary lunch at the Angel Hotel. The tablet is now in the Helston Museum.

By the time of the withdrawal of passenger trains, Helston station was the focal point of numerous local bus services. Prior to the departure of the morning connection for the 'Cornish Riviera Express', Western National buses provided connections at the station from and to Penzance (via Porthleven and via Godolphin); Falmouth (via Mabe and via Constantine); St Ives (summer only); Gunwalloe; Kuggar; The Lizard; Gillan; Coverack, St Keverne and Porthallow; Camborne; Redruth; and Lowertown. In 2012 most (but not all) of these villages and towns still enjoy regular bus services to Helston provided mainly by First Devon & Cornwall Ltd and Western Greyhound Ltd, and Helston is now served by a regular service to/from Truro, which it never enjoyed until some decades after the closure of the railway.

In the June 1887 edition of 'Bradshaw' a passenger service of five trains each way daily was advertised, but by the following month this had been augmented by an additional early-evening train each way. The Sunday service was replaced by a bus service in 1910. The basic timetable changed little throughout the history of the line. The final winter service (September-November 1962) showed eight trains to Helston and seven to Gwinear Road; on summer Saturdays in 1962 there were 13 and 10 trains respectively. Although connections were not provided at Gwinear Road with all expresses, Helston enjoyed good connections with the 'Cornish Riviera Express' from its inception until passenger services were withdrawn on the branch. From 5 November 1962 the 'Cornish Riviera' ceased to call at Gwinear Road and a stop at Redruth (with a Western National bus connection to Helston) was inserted in the schedule instead. Proposals to close Gwinear Road were published in the latter part of 1963 and were approved by the Minister of Transport in August 1964. The station closed from 5 October 1964, at the same time as many other intermediate stations on the Cornish main line.

Unlike many branches in Devon and Cornwall, Helston did not normally enjoy the benefit of through coaches to and from London. However, as Peter Semmens states in *The Heyday of GWR Train Services*,

OUR LOCAL EXPRESS
from Helston to Gwinear Road

The Cynicus Publishing Co Ltd (of Tayport in Fife) produced cards such as these, which were personalised for different local railways; this one is personalised to show 'Our Local Express from Helston to Gwinear Road'. *Original postcard in author's collection*

OUR LOCAL EXPRESS
HELSTON TO GWINEAR ROAD

Donald McGill is more famous for his 'saucy' seaside postcards, but also produced cards personalised for local railways. Here is his version of 'Our Local Express Helston to Gwinear Road'. *Helston Museum*

Helston enjoyed the facility of through services to and from Paddington on some summer Saturdays in 1939. Study of an appendix to the GWR 1938 working summer timetable indicates that on Saturdays the 10.35am from Paddington included up to five coaches for Helston, and that two coaches from Helston were attached at Gwinear Road to the up 9.45am service from St Ives (due into Paddington at 4.50pm).

Three locomotives per day were used on the branch during the final years of passenger services. One was stabled at Helston overnight and the other two were supplied by Penzance shed (83G) in the early morning and at midday. In later years trains were usually composed of two GWR non-corridor Brake Composite coaches, although on summer Saturdays three or four coaches were generally provided. Two 'B sets', each made up of two non-corridor Composite coaches built in 1930/31, were specially designated Helston 1 (W6445W and W6446W) and Helston 2 (W6464W and W6461W) on the outer ends of the coaches, but towards the end these were replaced or augmented by numerous other generally non-corridor coaches. Special corridor trains of approximately six coaches were run three times per annum in connection with the Royal Naval Air Station at Culdrose (HMS *Seahawk*) on the southern outskirts of Helston, but none was sent down the branch after 1962.

Rumours of the impending closure of the Helston branch to passengers began to circulate in the autumn of 1961. The statutory closure notices indicating the intention of the British Transport Commission (BTC) to shut the line and inviting representations to the Transport Users Consultative Committee for the South West (TUCC) were posted in November 1961. Numerous objections were lodged, and the committee held a full-day hearing in the Guildhall in Helston on Thursday 8 February 1962 under the chairmanship of Major General Abraham CBE. Among the objectors were Helston Borough Council; Kerrier Rural District Council; West Penwith RDC; Camborne-Redruth Urban District Council; the National Farmers Union; Cornwall Holiday & Tourist Association; and numerous parish councils and associations.

Concern was expressed, as happened at many similar closure inquiries throughout the UK at the time, about the opening statement by the Chairman that the committee would not take account of any criticism of the financial figures produced by the BTC, especially when he stated that 'in the Committee's experience (any) estimates had usually proved too low. He accepted the BTC's estimate of projected savings of £9,077 per annum as a minimum.' This figure included estimates (on a 40-year-life basis) of the annual renewal costs of a locomotive (£311pa) and four coaches (£438pa), and staff costs attributable to the passenger services of £12,839. As was common at the time, no consideration was given to reducing costs by staff or other savings, or of attracting more passengers by closing Gwinear Road and extending services to Camborne, this latter suggestion having been proposed by the Camborne Chamber of Commerce as long ago as 1908. After listening to the representations, and to responses from the BTC representatives and representatives of the Western National Omnibus Co Ltd, the committee approved the following resolution by a majority of 6 to 3.

'That in view of:-
a) the fact that so few residents on the Helston and Lizard peninsula now use the Helston/Gwinear Road branch, and that alternative services between Helston and Camborne/Redruth are at present working below capacity;
b) the fact that such a very small proportion of tourists to The Lizard peninsula now use the Gwinear Road/Helston branch and that although the number of

tourists is increasing year by year the small number of these using the branch is actually decreasing;
c) the fact that the BTC has promised to provide extra buses to connect with trains at Camborne and Redruth on Saturdays throughout the summer when tourist traffic is especially heavy; and
d) the fact that arrangements to be made under the BTC's proposals for the carriage of flowers and perishables appear reasonable
This Committee recommend the BTC's proposals be accepted.'

The branch, together with the Chacewater-Newquay line, was omitted from the maps advertising 'Holiday Run-About Tickets' in the summer of 1962. Despite a deputation of MPs having a meeting with the Minister of Transport, Ernest Marples, he confirmed that the closure should proceed, and the BTC announced that it would close 'as and from November 5th 1962'.

When Ernest Marples announced his consent to the proposed closure in the summer of 1962 a local businessman of standing – Pearce Gilbert –

The last trains on the branch ran on Saturday 3 November 1962. The weather was a mixture of heavy showers and sunny periods, and this photograph shows the 4.10pm departure. The tail light and the wet platform perhaps epitomise the sadness of the day. *Author*

commemorated with sadness the decision with a poem in the *Helston & District Free Gazette* – addressed to his former comrade on Mylor gun-site, Ernest Marples – which is reproduced here:

Lifeline...

Said Truthall Halt to Helston Town
The Minister has got me down,
Said Helston Town to Truthall Halt
This bitter blow is all your fault;
But not at all said Praze-an-Beeble
To say a thing like that is feeble,
Indeed this thunderbolt has fallen
Because of naughty Nancy Gollan.
Said Nancy – Fancy, well I'm blow'd,
Nobody's mentioned Gwinear Road –
That grim Sahara – vast, immense
From Waiting Room to gloomy gents!

WE SAY MODERNISE, NOT FINALISE

There being no Sunday service, the last passenger train ran on Saturday 3 November, and I enjoyed the dubious privilege of travelling on the last service. Ironically, the close proximity of Guy Fawkes Night resulted in the funeral rites resembling to some extent the festivities that had accompanied the opening 75 years earlier, and the last train arrived at Helston greeted by the sounds of fog detonators, fireworks, railway whistles, bugles and singing. Former boys of Helston Grammar School wore full mourning attire, including top hats, and a Mr B. Nicholas portrayed Dr Beeching, Chairman of the BTC, carrying a giant axe on his shoulder. Also wearing a top hat and morning dress but carrying an auctioneer's 'For Sale' board was Mr J. Jones, a Camborne solicitor and Clerk of Crowan Parish Council. 'Auld Lang Syne' was sung by the passengers at Praze, Nancegollan and Helston. On this sad occasion, the Helston magistrates allowed an extension of the licensing hours of the refreshment room by 1½ hours until 10.30pm.

The last train was made up of six coaches and was hauled by No D6312. Other locomotives on the branch that day were Nos D6308 and D6339, the latter carrying the correct 2C61 headcode. About 300 passengers made their last journey to Gwinear Road, where connections were made with the 8.50pm Penzance-Paddington service (hauled by 'Warship' Class No D844 *Spartan*) and the 2.30pm Paddington-Penzance (hauled by No D814 *Dragon*). The train arrived back at Helston at 9.59pm, 9 minutes late according to the timetable that was to cease to have effect immediately thereafter. The last train carried a wreath presented by boys of Helston Grammar School bearing the words 'In loving memory of the Helston-Gwinear Road express'. The last train was driven by Driver J. Ellis of St Ives, with Mr A. Rowe as second man, with whom Dr Michael (of Lismore) and his daughter travelled in the cab from Gwinear Road.

Dr Michael, a local general practitioner, had for many years been the railway employees' instructor in first aid. Despite attempts by some passengers and enthusiasts to seek to board the train back to Gwinear Road, the empty stock departed with no passengers at 10.14pm to the accompaniment of further fog detonators.

Pearce Gilbert again commemorated this important landmark in the history of the town in the *Helston Free Gazette*:

R.I.P.

Goodbye my little puff-puff –
The one propell'd by steam,
The Pundits say you didn't pay
So now you're just a dream.

The majesty of Kendall,
The voice of old Jack Hawes –
The 'Praze, Praze, Praze' of balmy days
Defy the Marples claws.

Farewell my little choo-choo,
The thrill of childhood days;
Alas, alack – we'll soon be back
To butts and donkey-shays!

The Helston line was the first branch in Cornwall to lose its passenger service since before the Second World War. It was not strictly a victim of the infamous Beeching Report – *The Reshaping of British Railways* – as it featured in Section 6 of the Report under the heading of 'Passenger Services under Consideration for Withdrawal before the Formulation of the Report'. As the Report was not published until 1963, the entry was marked with an asterisk to indicate that the withdrawal of services had already been implemented.

The Helston branch may have been the first in Cornwall to close, but it was quickly followed by the complete withdrawal of goods and passenger services on the Plymouth-Tavistock-Launceston line (29 December 1962) and between Chacewater and Newquay (2 February 1963). The line between Lostwithiel and Fowey closed in January 1965, and that between Bodmin Road, Bodmin General and Padstow followed two years later.

On the Helston branch a goods service of two trains each way daily (only one on Saturdays) survived after 1962, and Praze, Nancegollan and Helston remained open for goods and parcels traffic for almost two years. However, the branch was closed completely 'as and from October 5th 1964'. The last goods train officially ran on Friday 2 October, hauled by No D6324, but the same locomotive returned on Friday 9 October to collect 12 wagons remaining on the line. Goods traffic on the branch over the years had included coal – the Helston Gas Company even had its own wagons in the early days – as well as cattle, serpentine rock, potatoes, flowers, broccoli and even rabbits. A number of ventilated goods vans were actually fitted with roof brackets to carry destination boards with the legend 'Rabbit Traffic Helston to Sheffield' in the 1920s and 1930s. In 1938, for example, a GWR Siphon was included (as required) in the 12.15 Penzance-Crewe (Mail) and returned (attached at Bristol) with the 05.30 Paddington-Penzance (Mail).

An assurance was given by the Parliamentary Secretary to the Minister of Transport that the track would not be removed without the consent of the Minister and without prior notice being given to the Borough Council, but a start was made in tearing up the lines less than eight months later, in April 1965, without notice. In the previous month, on 12 March, the last ever train had visited the terminus at Helston hauled by No D6310 to remove the engine road points, which were needed elsewhere.

Gwinear Road station closed from 5 October 1964, and its famous wide level crossing gates were replaced in November 1965 by the first automatic level crossing barriers in Cornwall.

Since closure, the site of Helston station has been redeveloped for housing and a new road, but the old goods shed and a small piece of the platform have been incorporated in a sheltered housing scheme. The trackbed from the station for the first half-mile towards Gwinear Road has now totally disappeared under the Water-ma-Trout industrial estate, but thereafter it has not been interrupted as far as Nancegollan. Industrial units have been built on the site of Nancegollan station and goods yard, a bungalow has been built at Praze, and the trackbed between Praze and Crowan now forms a tarmac farm road. Save for remains of the platforms, nothing survives of the 'fine station' at Gwinear Road that had so impressed the *Western Daily Mercury* in 1887.

The identity of the locomotive that hauled the first train is unknown, and neither its number nor name (if any) is mentioned in contemporary reports. However, it is likely that it was a 0-6-0ST of the '850' Class, and there is evidence of the use of these locomotives (including Nos 859, 992, 1935, 1943 and 1973) on the branch in the 1890s and 1900s. However, two specific locomotives are believed to have been designed by William Dean for use on the Helston and St Ives lines, because both routes were subject to weight and sharp curve restrictions. Originally built at Swindon in 1890 with saddle tanks and a 0-4-2T wheel arrangement, they were rebuilt in 1895 as 0-4-4Ts with side tanks, and it is in this form that photographs exist of Nos 34 and 35 in the early 1900s. Less unusual were the 0-4-2Ts of Class '517' (built by the GWR between 1868 and 1885) and the 2-4-0T 'Metro' tanks, which operated many services in the first two decades of the 20th century. There are reports of

The demolition team between Praze and Nancegollan.
The late Fred Ivey

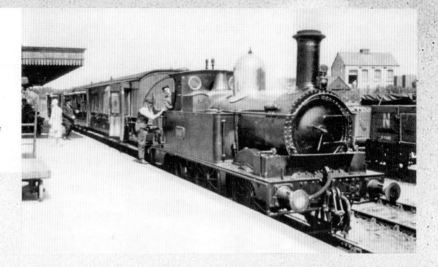

Immaculate Class '517' 0-4-2T No 1467 stands at Helston. The locomotive was built at the GWR's Wolverhampton works in 1883 as one of a class that eventually numbered 156, some of which operated on the Helston branch during the early decades of the 20th century. *Helston Museum*

the use of at least Nos 218, 529, 569, 571, 1163, 1431, 1466, 1467, 1481 and 1487 on the line, and No 1158 was allocated to Helston shed in 1921.

However, from the mid-1900s these 0-4-2Ts and 2-4-0Ts shared services with 2-6-2Ts of Class '44XX' (built by the GWR between 1904 and 1906 and originally numbered 115/3101-3110). Under the 1912 GWR renumbering scheme, these locomotives became Nos 4400-4410, but it will have been a locomotive bearing

its original number that features in a photograph in *The Railway Magazine* dated October 1911. A photograph of No 4404 at Helston is the only other print that I have seen of a Class '44XX' locomotive operating on the branch, but between 1906 and the mid-1930s every member of the class was shedded at some time at Helston, St Ives or Penzance, and was likely to have been used on the branch. Over the years the '44XXs' were joined and ultimately replaced by the more numerous

'45XX' locomotives with larger driving wheels, and also joined in the 1950s by their Class '4575' relations with greater water capacity and tapered side tanks.

The 0-4-2Ts and 2-4-0Ts also shared services with steam 'railmotors', self-contained steam-driven coaches suitable for use on lightly loaded services, which could reverse quickly as soon as the driver had walked from one end to the other. Railmotors operated on the Helston branch from 1905 until the 1920s, providing through services to destinations beyond Gwinear Road including Truro and Newquay. Railmotors Nos 25, 38, 61, 63, 72, 77, 90 and 96 are known to have been allocated to Helston, and others allocated to Penzance are likely to have visited the branch.

Given that 0-4-2Ts had operated the branch earlier in the century, it was perhaps not surprising that the GWR should experiment with new 0-4-2Ts of Class '48XX' (later Class '14XX') when they were introduced from 1932. They were a modern version of the '517' Class, and there is photographic evidence of at least one member of the class (No 4868) operating to Helston in June 1936 when only a few months old. The experiment was not successful, and the class was soon transferred away and duties taken over exclusively by Class '45XX' and (later) also by Class '4575' 'Prairie' tanks. Together they provided motive power for almost the whole of the line's remaining history, being replaced by D63XX (Class 22) diesel-hydraulic Bo-Bo locomotives in 1962, shortly before the withdrawal of passenger services. The monopoly of steam was broken in the spring of 1962, and the diesels took over all services from the beginning of the 1962 summer timetable. Some Class 22 locomotives operated on the branch within weeks of their delivery from the manufacturers. 'Prairie' tanks regularly employed on the branch after nationalisation included the prototype No 4500, as well as Nos 4505/9, 4525, 4537, 4540/5/7/8/9, 4561/3/4/6/8, 4570/1/4/7, 4587/8, 5508, 5515, 5537, 5545 and 5562. Two of these, Nos 4566 and 4588, have been preserved, and I am the proud owner of a cabside number plate from No 4566, purchased from British Railways for 2s 6d in 1962.

Ironically, it was only during the final months that an 0-6-0PT made a rare if not unique visit to Helston, when No 9748 was probably substituted for a failed diesel.

Theoretically, Class '43XX' 2-6-0 and '51XX' 2-6-2T locomotives could be specially authorised as far as Nancegollan, but I have seen no evidence of any such locomotives actually appearing. Thence to Helston, only locomotives of 'yellow' classification were permitted.

Although there were calls at the TUCC closure meeting for modern diesel multiple units (DMUs) to be introduced on the branch with a view to reducing costs and perhaps thereby saving the passenger services, no DMU ever ventured onto the branch before closure. In its evidence to the TUCC, the BTC stated that 'careful consideration had been given to the possibility of making the passenger train services remunerative by the introduction of diesel units operated under the cheapest working methods possible', but claimed that 'the movements costs of a service of this nature would total approximately £16,700 per annum apart from station costs etc. and that ... it would not be possible to provide a service on an economic basis.' These figures could not be challenged before the TUCC. However, in his book *The Rural Transport Problem*, published in 1963, David St John Thomas analysed the figures produced by the BTC, and questioned in particular the estimated DMU costs of £16,700 in the light of comparative estimates of £19,000 and £15,250 respectively produced by BTC for the 24-mile-long Exe Valley and 34-mile-long Launceston branches. With the use of a single DMU or a single loco-hauled train and a slightly amended timetable, he calculated that the annual loss could have been reduced to less than £2,000. Perhaps the branch could even have made a profit if new traffic had been attracted by marketing of the new service and if trains had been diverted from Gwinear Road to Camborne.

When the last piece of track was removed by the demolition contractors in 1965, I doubt that anyone would have ever imagined that trains would return. At that time there was no thought of running the line as a private preserved railway, as such schemes were then in their infancy. Narrow gauge lines such as the Talyllyn and the Ffestiniog had opened in Wales, but only a few attempts had been made to follow the example of the Bluebell Railway in Sussex to operate standard gauge lines for tourists. Since then, similar preserved lines have successfully been reopened in Devon and Cornwall, including the Bodmin & Wenford Railway, the Dart Valley Railway, the Paignton & Dartmouth Railway and the Plym Valley.

However, in 1994, 30 years after the last piece of track had been removed from the Helston branch, a local former British Rail employee and railway enthusiast announced a plan to reopen the whole line for regular daily services – despite development on the trackbed at Praze and Nancegollan – at an estimated cost of more than £3.5 million! According to the *Helston Packet* dated 7 April 1994 and *The West Briton* dated 18 August 1994, the promoters planned a metre-gauge railway to enable former Eastern Bloc rolling stock to be used and 'to allow two lines to be laid', and hoped not only to obtain European and Government grants but also to raise more than £90,000 per annum from a 4,000-square-foot Railway Heritage Centre. It was not, however, clear whether British Rail had any intention of reopening a station at Gwinear Road or of stopping trains there!

Not surprisingly, these grandiose plans came to nought, but they could have seriously damaged the prospects of a subsequent plan by keen and dedicated enthusiasts to reopen just part of the line as a purely tourist railway. The Helston Railway Preservation Society (HRPS) was formed in 2001 after two of its founding members walked along part of the abandoned and overgrown trackbed. With the support of the Trevarno estate, working parties started in 2005 to clear more than 40 years of vegetation – including gorse, trees and rhododendron bushes – on a section between Nancegollan and Truthall Halt. Track-laying commenced in 2006, and by the early summer of 2010 a new station had been completed at Trevarno. Two Ruston diesel shunters and a former Park Royal DMU were by then already in residence, and over the weekend of 25/26 July steam returned in the form of ex-Port of Par 0-4-0ST *Judy* kindly lent by the Bodmin & Wenford Railway. All this activity so impressed the judges on an unannounced visit that later in the year the railway was awarded the Ian Allan Publishing Heritage Railway of the Year Award. At a prestigious ceremony held at Merchant Taylors' Hall in the City of London in December, a plaque was duly presented to the HRPS by Pete Waterman OBE.

In short, in only six years HRPS members have laid more than a mile of track, constructed a completely new

station at Trevarno, replicated the metal footbridge on the public footpath that crosses the line at Tregadjack (on the Trevarno estate) and run both steam- and diesel-hauled trains. The Society has aspirations to extend the line over the Cober Viaduct to the edge of the Water-ma-Trout industrial estate in Helston. It is particularly appropriate that a station should – at last – be built at Trevarno, the former home of William Bickford-Smith MP, who had been the Chairman of the Company in 1882 when the prospectus for the original shares was issued. More details of this leap of faith in restoring part of the line are to be found towards the end of this book, which is dedicated – to repeat the words on the ceremonial street arches in 1882 – to 'The Success of the Helston Railway'.

The challenge faced by the Helston Railway Preservation Society and its supporters is clear here; at the site of what is now Trevarno station, Clif Walker attacks the undergrowth with shears in 2002. *Stuart Walker*

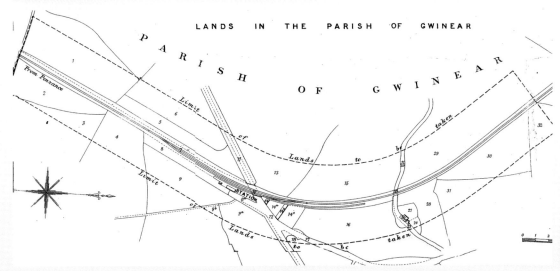

LANDS IN THE PARISH OF GWINEAR

A simple station comprising a platform on the single track West Cornwall Railway is known to have existed at Gwinear Road from 1852, as seen here, long before the arrival of the Helston branch.

GWR GWINEAR ROAD STATION

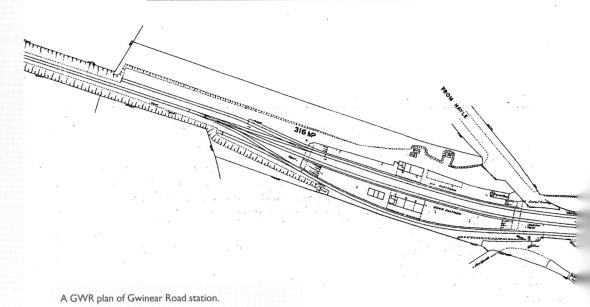

A GWR plan of Gwinear Road station.

Major enlargement and rebuilding was required to produce the 'fine station' commended by a local newspaper in 1887. This photograph of Gwinear Road station must date from the year of opening or very soon thereafter. It can be dated by the pristine state of the station buildings, signal box and level crossing gates, and by the mixed-gauge track on the main lines. In the Helston branch platform, the Helston locomotive stands for a posed photograph with its crew and no fewer than eight station staff, two of whom stand on or dangerously close to the down main line. Gwinear Road was rebuilt as a passing place in preparation for the opening of the Helston branch and remained so until the main line was doubled to the east towards Camborne in 1900 and to the west towards Hayle in 1915. The mixed gauge was a consequence of the West Cornwall Railway having built the line from Penzance to Truro to standard gauge in 1852 and Brunel's broad gauge having been added in 1866/67. This enabled trains from both the GWR and WCR to run through from Truro to provide through services from London to Penzance. The broad gauge was finally abandoned in May 1892 and it was in anticipation of its abolition that the Helston Railway was designed and authorised as a standard gauge line. *Helston Museum*

2nd Class single ticket issued on 30 September 1964 at St Erth, immediately before the closure of Gwinear Road.

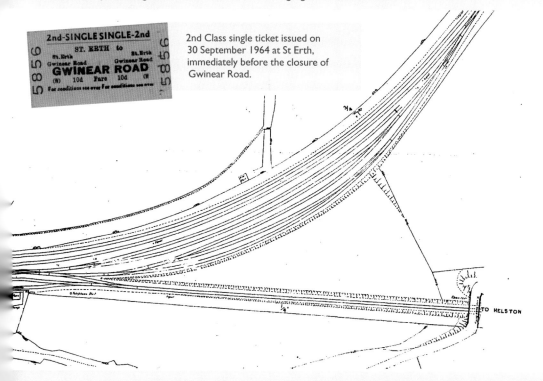

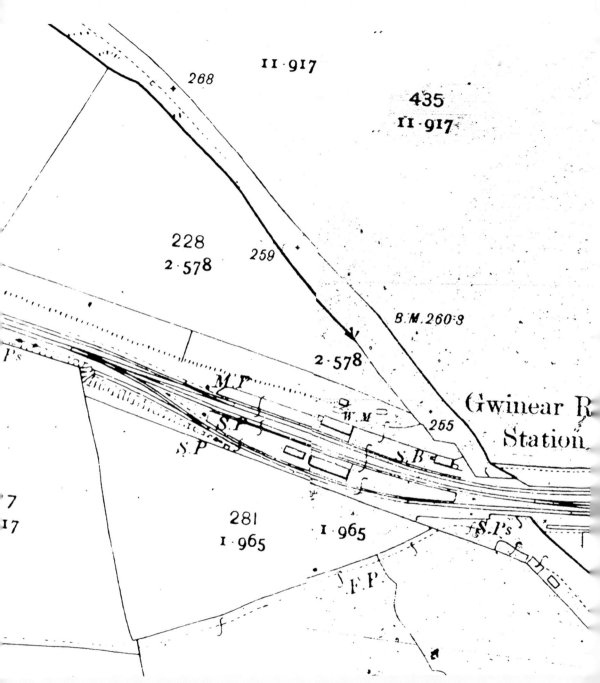

Gwinear Road in the early years of the 20th century. *Crown Copyright*

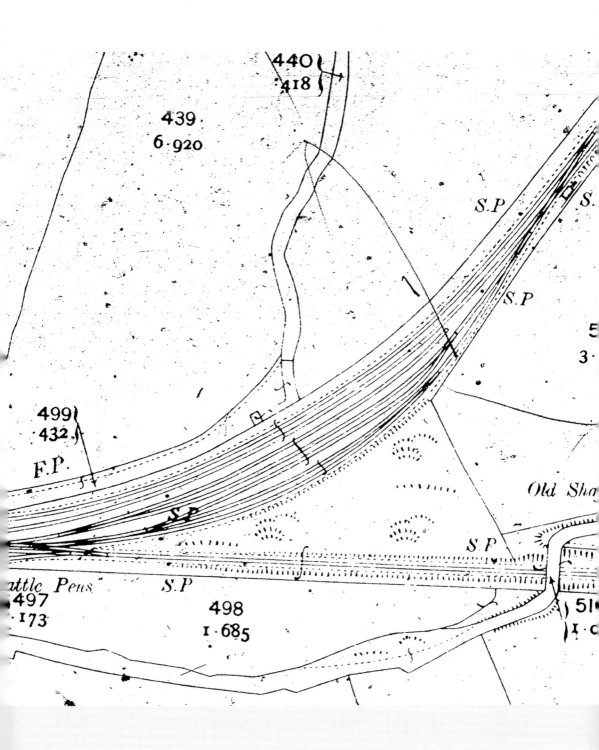

440
418

439
6·920

499
432

F.P.

499
432

S.P

S.P

S.P

S.P

S.P

S.P

Old Sha

attle Pens
497
·173

S.P

498
1·685

51
1·0

Looking west from the footbridge, probably in the 1920s or 1930s, the paintwork on the station buildings leaves much to be desired, although pride by station staff can be discerned from the flower bed on the extreme right of the photograph on the up main-line platform. Close examination of the photograph shows that the covered truck has not been abandoned on the up main but is being shunted, possibly on to rear of the Helston train.

Looking east on the same date, the milepost on the up platform indicates that Gwinear Road is 316 miles from Paddington (via Bristol). By now a footbridge spans the main lines, and beyond it can be seen the new signal box (Gwinear Road West), which replaced the 1887 box on the up side in 1915. The footbridge was erected before that date.

By the latter part of the 1950s the new diesels were sharing duties with steam locomotives. On 19 September 1959 'County' Class No 1023 *County of Oxford* approaches Gwinear Road at the head of the up 'Royal Duchy', comprising an almost complete rake of smart BR stock in chocolate and cream livery. Sadly, *County of Oxford* does not carry the 'Royal Duchy' headboard, and a Full Brake in BR maroon has been included in the train immediately behind the loco. *County of Oxford* was shedded at Truro (83F) between 1951 and 1959, and was almost always turned it out in exemplary condition. *P. Q. Treloar*

By the later 1950s the 'Cornish Riviera' would most probably have been hauled by a 'Castle' Class 4-6-0 locomotive, or possibly by a smaller 'Hall', but no longer by a BR Standard 'Britannia' 'Pacific'. These 4-6-2 locomotives operated in Cornwall for a short period after they were built in 1951 (Nos 70015-70024 in particular), and No 70019 *Lightning* was the first to haul the 'Cornish Riviera' in Cornwall in August 1951. On 10 April 1952 this down principal express of the day is hauled by No 70024 *Vulcan*, which at this date was only about five months old and had been allocated to Plymouth Laira shed (83D) less than three months previously. The 10-coach train has not yet been provided with BR Mk 1 coaches, first introduced in 1951, and is formed of ex-GWR rolling stock, including behind the locomotive two Hawksworth vehicles, the last GWR design. The branch train to provide the connection to Helston from the 'Cornish Riviera' can just be seen approaching above the third coach of the main-line train. *B. A. Butt*

Right: In about 1958 there are no new BR Mk I coaches in the formation of this down local train, hauled by 'Grange' Class No 6808 *Beenham Grange*. The 'Granges' were introduced by the GWR from 1936 and were similar to the 'Hall' Class but with smaller wheels. A substantial number were allocated to Cornish sheds throughout the life of the class, and *Beenham Grange* would have been a regular visitor to Gwinear Road as a Penzance engine between 1950 and 1962. *P. Q. Treloar*

G. W. R.

W. & S. Ltd.

GWINEAR ROAD

Below: By 1961 many local services in Cornwall had been handed over to diesel multiple units (DMUs). Providing a standard of comfort not matched in most modern DMUs rostered for much longer journeys, a three-car Swindon-built Cross Country Class 120 unit pauses at Gwinear Road forming a down local service on 22 September 1961. The headcode 2C73 on the rear of the unit presumably referred to its last up journey, but is a mystery. The Working Timetable of Passenger Trains in the Plymouth District for the period commencing September 1962 (a year later) suggests that it would have been carried by a train terminating at Saltash, but it seems more likely that this is the return working of a service to Plymouth that should correctly have displayed 2C74. *Author*

During the period between the withdrawal of passenger services to Helston in November 1962 and the closure of Gwinear Road station in October 1964, the down running-in board was altered to remove any reference to connections, and was in this condition when photographed on a wet day with D6325 adjacent. However, this has created another mystery, as the photograph of the preserved complete sign taken on 12 August 2011 shows no sign of any alterations. *Both author*

The pointwork leading to the branch can clearly be seen in this photograph of immaculate 'Castle' Class No 5053 *Earl Cairns* at the head of the 2.00pm Penzance-Crewe vans train on 29 April 1960. The locomotive is a credit to Plymouth Laira shed (83D), where it was allocated at the time. The Distant signal on the right has been pulled off to indicate a clear run past Gwinear Road East box. The bracket signal beside it (No 7 on the diagram) relates to an up loop provided to enable goods trains to be recessed and be overtaken by passenger trains. *R. C. Riley*

The Gwinear Road West Signal Box diagram shows that the up goods running loop had been removed before the closure of the box. The bracket signal seen in the photograph on page 47 – No 7 on the diagram – and the associated points (Nos 39, 40A and 40B) have been deleted. *Author's collection*

GWINEAR

SPA

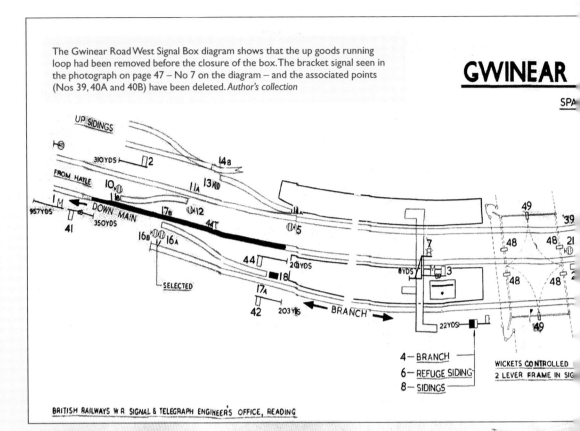

BRITISH RAILWAYS W R SIGNAL & TELEGRAPH ENGINEER'S OFFICE, READING

Gwinear Road West box and the famous level crossing gates can be seen in all their glory in this photograph taken on 8 September 1962. They look as if they have only recently been repainted, although within three years, in June 1965, they would be replaced by automatic lifting barriers. *Author*

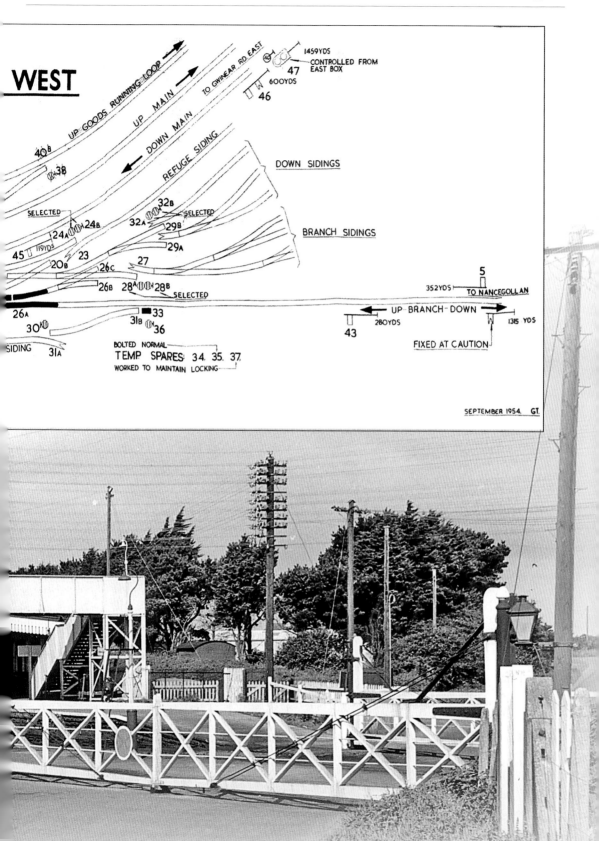

WEST

UP GOODS RUNNING LOOP

UP MAIN

TO GWINEAR RD EAST

DOWN MAIN

REFUGE SIDING

DOWN SIDINGS

BRANCH SIDINGS

1459YDS
47 — CONTROLLED FROM EAST BOX
46　600YDS

40B
38
SELECTED
32B
32A　SELECTED
24A　24B
29B
45　119YDS
29A
20B　26C　23
26B　28A　28B
27
26A　SELECTED
30
31B　33
SIDING　31A
36

5
352YDS　TO NANCEGOLLAN

UP-BRANCH-DOWN
280YDS
43　FIXED AT CAUTION　1315 YDS

BOLTED NORMAL
TEMP SPARES. 34. 35. 37.
WORKED TO MAINTAIN LOCKING

SEPTEMBER 1954. GT.

At the eastern end of Gwinear Road the main line from Camborne approached the station around a sharp right-hand curve and across the wide level crossing over the road between Carnhell Green and Gwithian. It is perhaps surprising that the station was not named Helston Road as this road is marked as 'To Helston' on early railway maps and does not lead directly to Gwinear! On 31 May 1960 an early 'Warship' Class (later Class 42) diesel-hydraulic, No D805 *Benbow*, arrives at Gwinear Road at the head of the down 'Cornish Riviera Express' carrying not only the traditional headboard but also the reporting number C30 and express discs. The early members of the class were not fitted with roller blinds for headcodes and carried when necessary GWR steam locomotive reporting numbers, which were limited to three panels and could not display the full code of 1C30. *Author*

The head code 1V86 on 'Warship' No D845 *Sprightly*
indicates that it was hauling an inter-regional express
when photographed at the same spot on 18 September
1961. Staff wait to cross the line with a traditional railway
barrow carrying post from the Helston branch for 'up
country'. *Sprightly* was the only 'Warship' to receive
a small yellow panel and a white strip above the cab
windows, and had been so adorned only in the previous
month. Subsequently, larger yellow panels were applied
until ultimately complete yellow fronts were settled upon
as a safety measure. *Author*

It was important that connections with main-line services
at Gwinear Road should be maintained. The 1962 Working
Timetable stressed, for instance, that the 1.15pm from
Helston 'must not be delayed' and required the 'working to
be given special consideration'. Back in 1904 a delay to the
up 6.00pm Mail train because of a staff failure (presumably
a signalling staff failure rather than a personal failing) led to
an official complaint from the Postmaster General, which
was passed on by the Divisional Superintendent & District
Goods Managers Office within the month!

After the closure of the branch and its exchange sidings, there was no longer any need for signal boxes at Gwinear Road other than to operate the level crossing and its protecting signals. Accordingly, Gwinear Road East Signal Box closed on 20 June 1965, and the West box closed on 31 October of the same year when automatic half-barriers – the first in Cornwall – came into use. On 29 July 1992 a Class 122 single-car unit in BR blue and grey livery crosses the level crossing and approaches the closed but clearly identifiable down platform while operating the 18.50 Exeter-Penzance service. In former days such a service would normally have been formed of at least five or six coaches hauled by an express locomotive. *Author*

The up platform is less well preserved, as can be seen in this 1994 photograph of a Class 47 in Parcels livery passing on an up postal train. *Author*

Above: Almost 20 years later, the scene has changed little. On 10 August 2011 a First Great Western High Speed Train led by Class 43 No 43183 leans to the curve while forming the 10.00 Penzance-Paddington service. The train is in immaculate condition – it is rare to see FGW's HSTs in anything but. Compared with 1962 (page 49), there are fewer fir trees in the background, but some have survived. In the summer of 1962 the up (Monday-Friday) 'Cornish Riviera' took 6hr 45min to travel from Penzance to Paddington (and almost 7hr 15min on Saturdays); by 2011 the 10.00 would reach Paddington in 5hr 24min, and the 'Cornish Riviera' (which now leaves Penzance earlier at 08.44) in 5 hours exactly.

The road is now much busier than in the 1960s, and the almost total absence of traffic in this picture is misleading. The T board, indicating the end of a speed restriction, relates to a temporary 25mph limit recently imposed in both directions because of worries about visibility at the crossing. Sadly, NetworkRail seems unaware of the correct spelling of 'Gwinear' (*inset*) – it is to be hoped that this error will be corrected without delay! *Both author*

Right: Turning to the east, the rear of Cross Country 'Voyager' unit No 221138 is seen on the same day forming the 09.40 Penzance-Manchester service. No sign remains of the former bustling goods yard, or the Helston branch, which used to pass to the right of the trees on the right of the photograph. The 09.40 is due into Manchester at 16.59. Two earlier Cross Country services from Penzance pass Gwinear Road heading for Birmingham and the north. *Author*

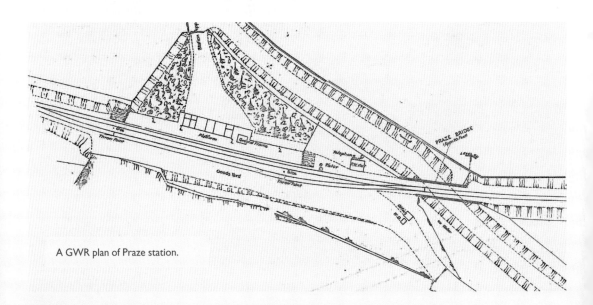

A GWR plan of Praze station.

This 1920s view (facing north-west) suggests that Praze provided little goods traffic to the national network, with only one goods wagon in the goods loop. The catch point blade, the end of which is just visible in the foreground, indicates that the loop has not yet been converted into a siding accessed only from the north.

The goods potential seems to have changed little by 11 July 1961, as No 4570 enters Praze heading for Helston with the 2.25pm service from Gwinear Road. However, the covered wagon now clearly stands in a siding. *Peter Gray*

Although the branch was to remain open for goods traffic until 1964, no goods traffic was on offer when the station was photographed facing south in August 1962. With closure to passengers already announced, it is perhaps not surprising that the station is not looking as smart as in the past. *Author*

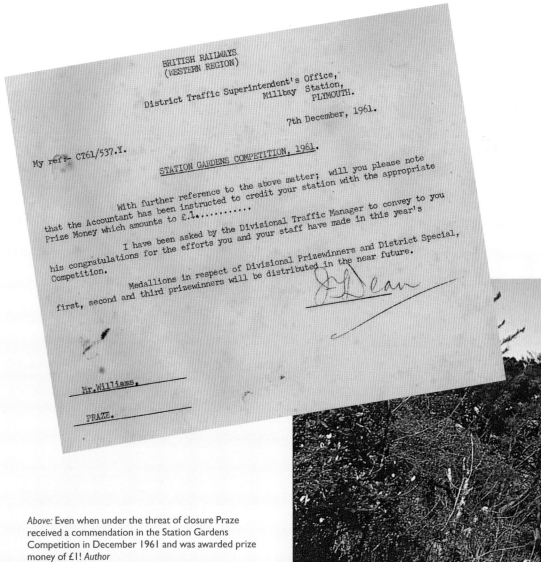

BRITISH RAILWAYS.
(WESTERN REGION)

District Traffic Superintendent's Office,
Millbay Station,
PLYMOUTH.

7th December, 1961.

My ref:- CT61/537.Y.

STATION GARDENS COMPETITION, 1961.

With further reference to the above matter; will you please note that the Accountant has been instructed to credit your station with the appropriate Prize Money which amounts to £.1...........

I have been asked by the Divisional Traffic Manager to convey to you his congratulations for the efforts you and your staff have made in this year's Competition.

Medallions in respect of Divisional Prizewinners and District Special, first, second and third prizewinners will be distributed in the near future.

Mr.Williams.

PRAZE.

Above: Even when under the threat of closure Praze received a commendation in the Station Gardens Competition in December 1961 and was awarded prize money of £1! *Author*

Right: Little remains at Praze to indicate the former presence of a railway other than the bridge supports for the former steel girder bridge over the Helston road. Perhaps the only common denominator in these two photographs, taken from the south in 1962 and 2011 respectively, is the Scots pine tree. This can be seen respectively to the right of the water tower and behind the modern house, which with its garden now occupies the whole site. *Both author*

Nancegollan

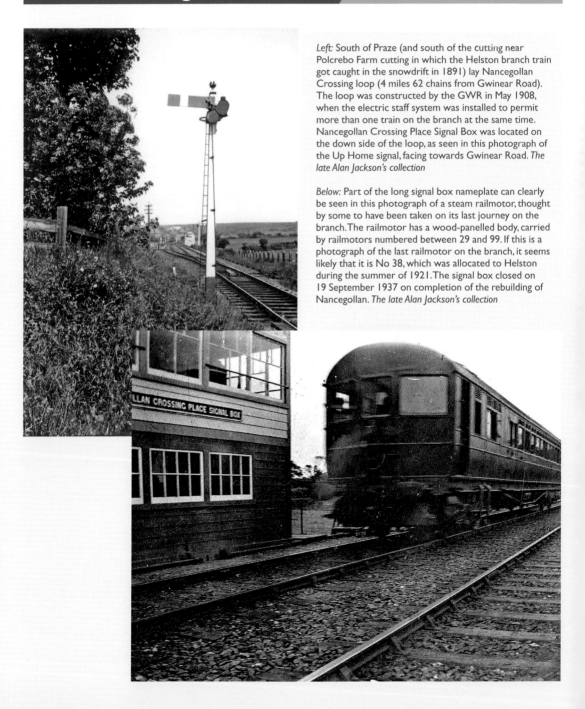

Left: South of Praze (and south of the cutting near Polcrebo Farm cutting in which the Helston branch train got caught in the snowdrift in 1891) lay Nancegollan Crossing loop (4 miles 62 chains from Gwinear Road). The loop was constructed by the GWR in May 1908, when the electric staff system was installed to permit more than one train on the branch at the same time. Nancegollan Crossing Place Signal Box was located on the down side of the loop, as seen in this photograph of the Up Home signal, facing towards Gwinear Road. *The late Alan Jackson's collection*

Below: Part of the long signal box nameplate can clearly be seen in this photograph of a steam railmotor, thought by some to have been taken on its last journey on the branch. The railmotor has a wood-panelled body, carried by railmotors numbered between 29 and 99. If this is a photograph of the last railmotor on the branch, it seems likely that it is No 38, which was allocated to Helston during the summer of 1921. The signal box closed on 19 September 1937 on completion of the rebuilding of Nancegollan. *The late Alan Jackson's collection*

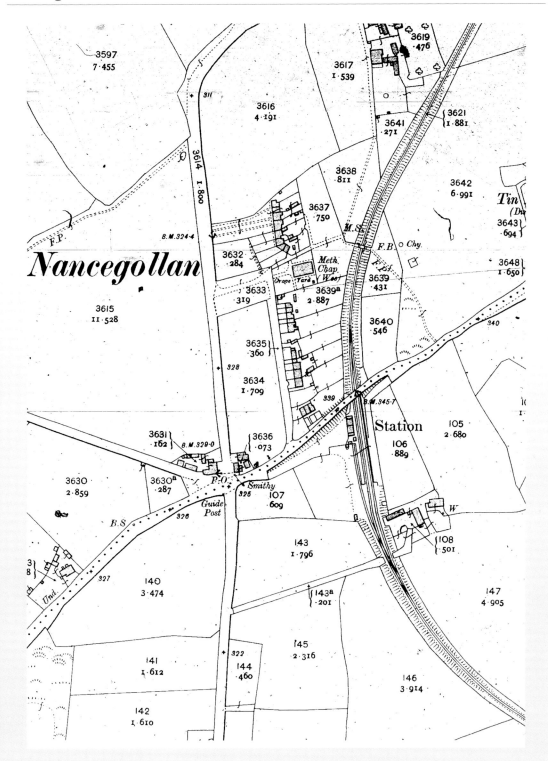

Nancegollan and its station. *Crown Copyright*

A GWR plan of Nancegollan station.

Below: Nancegollan station was a quarter of a mile south of Nancegollan Crossing Place; it is perhaps surprising that the GWR should have installed a loop there, as from the outset the layout at Nancegollan would have enabled such a loop to have been provided in the station itself (subject to the appropriate signalling arrangements). However, the Board of Trade inspecting officer, Colonel Rich, was unhappy about the provision of a loop on a line then intended to be operated on a one-engine-in-steam principle. Accordingly, he ordered that only one line – that on the right in this photograph looking towards Helston – be used by passenger trains and that the platform and line on the left should be used as a goods siding only. *Martin Matthews collection*

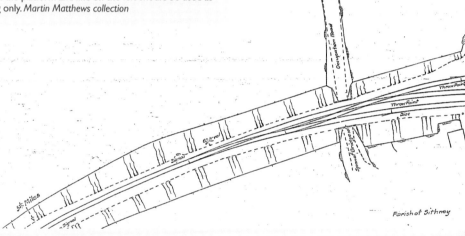

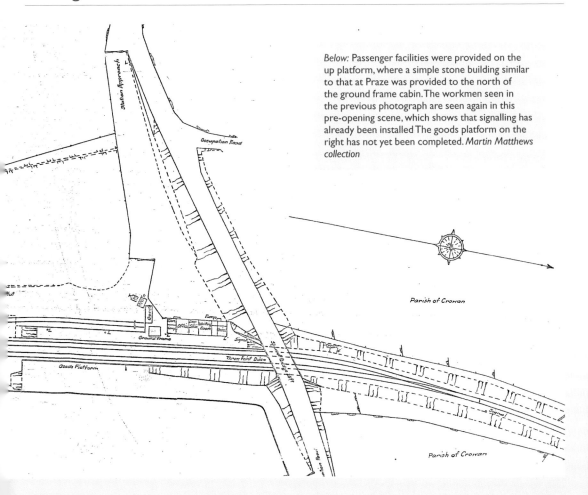

Below: Passenger facilities were provided on the up platform, where a simple stone building similar to that at Praze was provided to the north of the ground frame cabin. The workmen seen in the previous photograph are seen again in this pre-opening scene, which shows that signalling has already been installed The goods platform on the right has not yet been completed. *Martin Matthews collection*

Above: In this 1920s south-facing view the short goods platform in now in use, together with a south-facing goods siding partially behind the passenger platform. *Cornwall Council collection*

Below and opposite page: On rebuilding in 1937, new passenger facilities were constructed on the extended former goods platform, and the original brick building on the up side was replaced by a simple shelter to the south of the new signal box. At the same time the former siding on the up side was converted into a goods loop adjacent to a loading bank, and extra sidings were provided. These works necessitated the lengthening of the road bridge at the north end of the station, and the road was extended over the goods lines on a steel girder bridge. These features are clearly portrayed in these three photographs, taken in August 1962, showing the signal box, the 1937 station building on the down platform, and a general view of the station looking north. *All author*

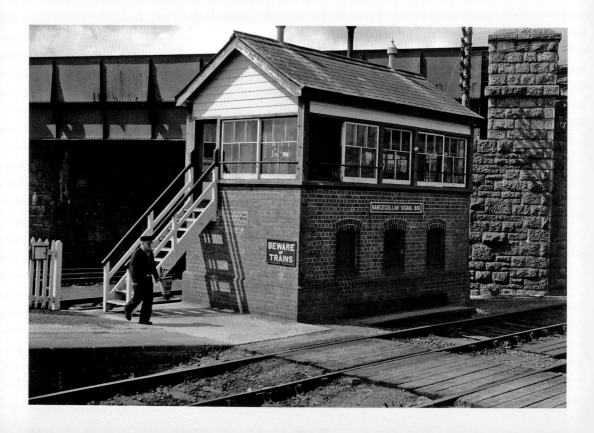

A Camping Coach was located at Nancegollan between 1958 and 1962, but more permanent was an old coach body from a Dean clerestory family saloon No 9025, built in 1903, which served as an office for a local silage merchant from 1946 until closure of the line. Flanked by an equally decrepit but younger flat-bed lorry, the old coach was photographed on 26 May 1963. By then the interior was no longer being used, but was still in good order. *The late Pat English*

Despite the demands of its busy goods yard and its staff having a duty to check and collect tickets on all southbound trains – Helston being an open station – the staff found time to tend their garden. So keen were they that the station regularly achieved success in the British Railways (Western Region) Station Gardens Competition as evidenced by this certificate showing Third Class awards in 1953/54/55 and 1961; a Special Class award in 1956; and a Second Class award in 1957. The award in 1961 is perhaps particularly significant as it demonstrates that staff morale had not been destroyed by the rumours of impending closure. *Helston Museum*

The Station Master at Nancegollan at the time of the awards was Stephen Jeffrey. He was also for many years Chairman of Kerrier District Council. *Helston Museum*

Demolition commenced in 1965, after closure to goods traffic in 1964. This photograph shows the signal protecting departure from the goods loop to the south, but the rusty state of the track indicates that there are no longer any movements to be authorised. *The late Fred Ivey*

Below: Not long afterwards the demolition men moved in – already the track has been lifted and the wooden shelter on the up platform demolished. *The late Fred Ivey*

Right: Fifty years later, little remains of the station itself, but the bridges at the north end bear witness to the former railway, despite the fact that the station site and the goods yard have been redeveloped as a light industrial estate. Ironically, one of the units is owned and occupied by a company (Trevarno Marquee & Event Hire) owned by Peter Bickford-Smith, whose great-grandfather William Bickford-Smith MP was Chairman of the Helston Railway Company at the time of the opening of the line. *Author*

William Bickford-Smith's father, George Smith LL.D, was a Director of the West Cornwall Railway from 1844 and its Vice-Chairman between 1859 and 1863. Peter is the proud owner of two West Cornwall Railway 1st Class passes – one in ivory and one in gold – issued to his great-great-grandfather. *Peter Bickford-Smith*

Right: The overbridge immediately south of Truthall Halt was also photographed (looking north) at the time of the opening of the line and, as at Prospidnick, the quality of the workmanship that so impressed the Board of Trade inspector in 1887 can be seen. Twenty years later Truthall Halt was constructed by the GWR immediately beyond the bridge on the right. *Martin Matthews collection*

Below: When it opened, the platform at Truthall Halt was long enough to accommodate two coaches, but later it was reduced to one coach in length. Opened on 1 July 1905, it comprised a typical GWR 'pagoda' shelter made of corrugated iron, but its cinder and sleeper platform was unusual in that it was buttressed by lengths of old Barlow rail used initially but unsuccessfully by the West Cornwall Railway. It was lit by an oil lamp on the platform, and by another at the entrance to the short path from the road, but the running-in board was not illuminated.

The halt changed little during its 55-year life. In these views taken on 30 August 1960, part of the gate leading to the entrance path can just be seen on the right behind the 'pagoda' shelter. *Both author*

Climbing away from the viaduct, the line eventually levelled out and crossed the road to Lowertown and an accommodation bridge of dressed granite. The substantial nature of the latter (on the left) can be seen in this photograph taken in 1994, 30 years after the line's closure.

As seen in the second photograph, the bridge now marks the end of the railway formation as the land thence towards Helston station has been redeveloped as a light industrial estate. Now more overgrown, the new 'end of line' is starkly portrayed, in a contrast between the newly built estate road and the abandoned trackbed. *Both author*

Opposite: inset: After Truthall Halt the line dropped down through rock cuttings to the largest and most expensive structure on the line, the Cober Viaduct. In this early postcard view of the viaduct, one of the two 0-4-4Ts, No 34 or 35, is seen heading for Gwinear Road. *Helston Museum*

Main picture: Looking towards Helston from the viaduct, the River Cober can be seen 90 feet below tumbling (to the right) down to Helston, the Loe Bar and the sea in Mount's Bay. *David Collings collection*

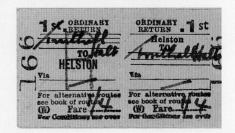

Above: The next, and penultimate, bridge before Helston was on overbridge on the outskirts of the town in an area with the unusual name of Water-ma-Trout. In 1962 an unidentified diesel-hydraulic loco passes the fixed Distant signal. The route of the railway at this point is now followed approximately by a road on the Water-ma-Trout Industrial Estate, which extends as far as the road to Lowertown, the line of which can be identified by the line of trees just above the rear coach. *Author*

Below: The formation of the branch lay on or just to the right of this spur road on the Water-ma-Trout Industrial Estate. The Lowertown road bridges lie in the trees behind the distant caravan. No signs remain of the former overbridge that stood at or immediately to the right of the spot from which this photograph was taken in November 2011. *Author*

Above: The bridge at Water-ma-Trout, described as Lower Tranneck Bridge on the original plans, is seen behind No D6310 and its train, the 9.50am service from Helston to Gwinear Road, on 9 July 1962, hauled by Class 22 No D6310. *Author*

Below: After Water-ma-Trout, the line headed towards the bridge at the entrance to Helston station itself. On the left of this up goods service hauled by No D6349 can be seen the sign requiring all down goods trains not fitted with continuous brakes to stop to pin down brakes before approaching the terminus. The headcode for passenger trains on the branch shows that this scene was captured before November 1962. *Author*

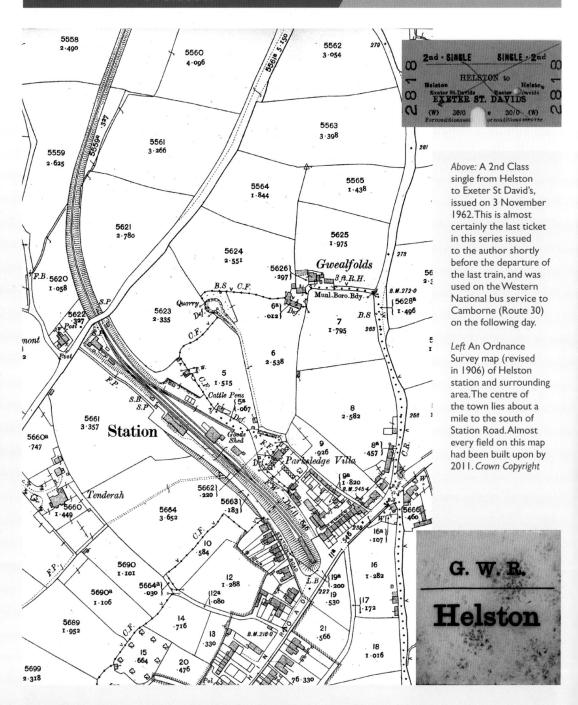

Above: A 2nd Class single from Helston to Exeter St David's, issued on 3 November 1962. This is almost certainly the last ticket in this series issued to the author shortly before the departure of the last train, and was used on the Western National bus service to Camborne (Route 30) on the following day.

Left An Ordnance Survey map (revised in 1906) of Helston station and surrounding area. The centre of the town lies about a mile to the south of Station Road. Almost every field on this map had been built upon by 2011. *Crown Copyright*

The signal gantry allowing entry to Helston station frames No 4577 as it departs at the head of the Saturdays-only midday branch goods, probably in 1958 or 1959 when the locomotive was allocated to Penzance shed. This photograph is of particular interest because it shows the locomotive facing south, a very rare breach of the normal rule that engines on the branch must face towards Gwinear Road. *P. Q. Treloar*

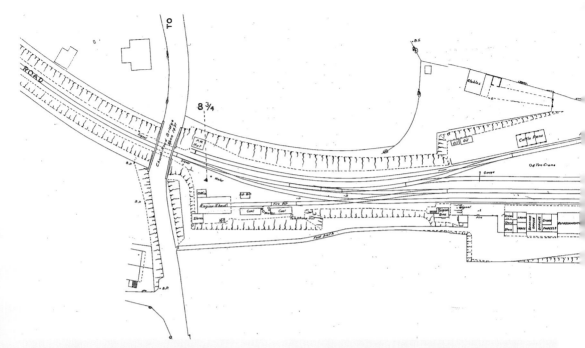

Below The layout and pointwork in the station can be observed in this view from the Church Hill overbridge. Before alterations to the layout were carried out in 1915, access to the engine shed was obtained from the running release road across the platform line by means of a diamond crossing, as in the plan above. This required a locomotive from the shed wishing to rejoin a train in the platform to carry out a complicated manoeuvre, and a new and more convenient arrangement was approved by the Board of Trade in 1915. *Helston Museum*

A GWR plan of Helston station. pre-1915

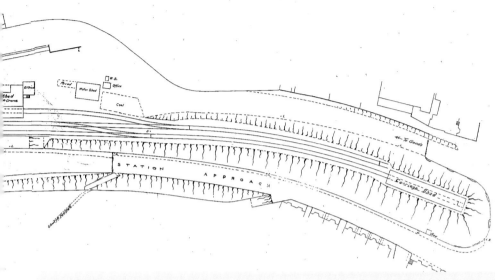

Below: The new layout is clearly shown in this 1920s view, which shows the stone siding on the left before its removal by the GWR. In the distance the carriage shed (see page 85) is conspicuous.

Above: The new arrangements involved a facing point on
the passenger platform line, and the engine shed spur was
graced with a full bracket signal rather than a shunting signal.
The signals can be glimpsed in this view of No 4564 leaving
Helston at the head of the 4.15pm service during the final
passenger years on 5 May 1961. Note the hopper wagon on
the stone siding. *Author*

Below: The stone siding is shown here in greater detail.
An earlier siding at this location had been removed by the
GWR in 1932, but it was reinstated in the 1950s to cater
for serpentine stone traffic. *Author*

Above: On 30 June 1962 new Class 22 No D6345 is in charge of the 4.35pm Saturdays-only service, passing the same spot as No 4564 opposite. In both photographs the signalman has already returned the Starter signal to danger. *Author*

Below: The overbridge and cutting were filled in after closure and the land was sold to the local authority to enable a new road to be built. Station Road was formerly a private road in the ownership of the GWR, and terminated just beyond the station building; it is now a public highway and has been extended to join Church Hill just south of the former overbridge. In this 2011 photograph the wall on the right marks the former boundary of the railway land adjacent to the engine shed, while another distinguishing mark is the roof of the former goods shed that just projects above the sheltered housing bungalows. *Author*

Above and left: The water tower adjacent to the engine shed spur, Helston signal box and the bracket signals controlling the main line (right) and the engine shed spur (left) are bathed in sunlight in these views; the spur signal arm is slightly shorter than that for the passenger line. The signal box stands at the end of the platform. *Both author*

Opposite: Exit from Helston station was controlled by the Advance Starter in front of Church Hill overbridge. Shunting was controlled by a short shunting arm, which replaced in the early 1950s an ordinary arm adorned by a large 'S' symbol. In front of the signal post can be seen the milepost indicating 8¾ miles from Gwinear Road. *Author*

Above: The canopy over the platform is a prominent
feature in this staged photograph of the assembled staff,
taken probably about the end of the Victorian era. It would
have been of even more interest if the photographer had
included the whole of the branch engine – 0-4-4T No 35 –
but he has certainly captured the pride of the staff in their
employment by the GWR. *Helston Museum*

Below: Some 60 years later, in 1962, viewed from beyond
the goods shed, an early D63XX diesel-hydraulic, without
headcode panels, has pulled further down the platform.
The train is connecting with numerous Western National
Bristol double-decker buses in the station approach. That
closest to the station building is on Route 27 to The Lizard,
a successor to the GWR motor bus service referred to
later. *Author*

Above: The station can be seen here more clearly in the background beyond smart No 4588, which is reversing towards the end of the line, possibly to collect coaches berthed at the buffer stops. No 4588 was based at Penzance shed between March 1959 and September 1961. *Author*

Below: By 2011 the view had been transformed. On the left a small remnant of the platform has survived, while the goods shed has been sympathetically adapted as the common areas of a sheltered housing scheme known as Hens Horn Court. The HRPS hopes to erect a plaque on this building in 2012 to mark the 125th anniversary of the opening of the railway. *Author*

Top: The station platform and building changed little during the life of the branch. From the approach road, which rose at a slight gradient from its junction with Godolphin Road, the station building presented an imposing appearance. Constructed of local dressed granite and with four massive chimneys, it stood to the right of the approach road and to the left of the running line. There was a full-length canopy over the platform, and a slightly shorter one on the road side. In practice, at least in later years, few passengers entered the station through the ticket office from the roadside, most preferring to enter via the (always open) gate beyond the telephone kiosk. It is hard to miss the GWR sign advertising the presence of a Refreshment Room at the station, which unusually was privately operated. *Author*

Above: The 2011 scene has less architectural merit. The remains of the platform can be glimpsed on the right, but sadly the sturdy station building has been replaced by uninspiring bungalows and an extension to Station Road, the uneven surface of which probably bears witness to its construction on infilled land where the engine shed formerly stood. *Author*

Beyond the station platform the line continued for about 200 yards on an embankment steadily increasing in height to the very end of the line, the most southerly piece of railway track in Great Britain. From the date of opening until the mid-1950s the line ended in a carriage shed about 100 feet in length, constructed of wood with a shallow clerestory roof. Luckily the shed was photographed shortly before its demolition. *Both the late Pat English*

Coaching stock continued to be berthed there even after the carriage shed had been demolished. Although the geographical importance of this piece of line on the railway map would not have been appreciated by most motorists driving past in Godolphin Road, few could miss it when coaches were berthed there as they were generally left hard up to the buffer stops, almost overhanging the public highway. The coaches are very conspicuous in these two 1962 photographs taken from the east and west respectively in Godolphin Road. A 'To Passenger Station' sign, albeit without a directional arrow, at the junction of Godolphin Road and Station Road attempts to be helpful. *Both author*

Thirty years later, in 1994, the embankment is overgrown but otherwise unchanged, and the view remains the same today. *Author*

Even before the publication of the infamous Beeching Report – *The Reshaping of British Railways* – in 1963, numerous branch lines throughout Great Britain were being closed by British Railways, but none had suffered that fate in Cornwall. However, rumours that the Helston branch was under threat began to circulate in 1961 and posters giving statutory notice of the British Transport Commission's intention to withdraw passenger services went up in November 1961. This poster was photographed at Gwinear Road. *Author*

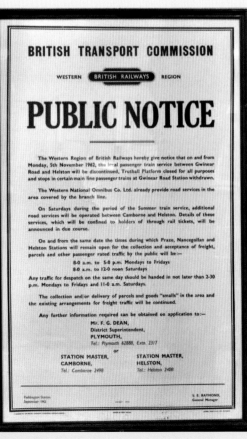

After the Transport Users Consultative Committee met in February 1962 and resolved to approve the proposals, a second poster announced that the local passenger service between Gwinear Road and Helston would be discontinued 'on and from Monday, 5th November 1962'. This poster was obtained from the British Railways poster store at Exeter St David's by the author and is now on loan to Helston Museum. No doubt because such notices lacked the attraction of pictorial posters, few have survived. *Author*

Table 102 **GWINEAR ROAD and HELSTON**

WEEK DAYS ONLY

Mls		am S		am	am	am S	am E	am S		pm S	pm S	pm E	pm S	pm E	pm S	pm E	pm S	pm S	pm		pm
—	**Gwinear Road** ... dep	6 15	..	7 45	8 30	10 22	10 55	11 5	..	12 37	1 46	2 10	2 20	4 11	4 30	5 0	5 24	7 4	8 10	..	9 50
2¾	Praze	6 23	....	7 55	8 38	10 30	11 3	11 13	....	12 45	1 54	2 17	2 28	4 19	4 38	5 8	5 32	7 12	8 18	....	9 58
5¼	Nancegollan ...	6 28	..	8 2	8 43	10 35	11 8	11 18	..	12 50	1 59	2 24	2 33	4 26	4 49	5 13	5 38	7 19	8 23	..	10 3
7	Truthall Platform ...	....	....	....	8 49	10 41	11 14	11 24	....	12 56	....	2 29	....	4 32	....	5 19	5 44	....	....	....	10 9
8¾	**Helston** ... arr	6 40	..	8 20	8 55	10 47	11 20	11 30	..	1 2	2 10	2 35	2 44	4 38	5 0	5 25	5 50	7 29	8 34	..	10 15
—	The Lizard ¶ .... arr	....	....	....	10 22	12 15	1 19	1 19	....	....	....	4 15	4 15	6 22	6 22	7 29	7 29	....	9 57	....	....

Miles		am S	am S	am E		am		am S		am S		am		pm		pm E	pm S		pm		pm	
	The Lizard ¶ ... dep	..	..	..	..	8B 3	..	..		10 25	..	10 25	..	1 22	..	..	..	..	5 11	..	7 32	..
—	**Helston** .... dep	5H45	7H50	7 45	....	9H50	....	10H22	....	12H 0	....	1 10	....	3 30	....	4 10	4 35	....	7 5	....	8 45	....
1½	Truthall Platform ...	..	..	7 51	..	..	..	..	..	..	..	..	..	3 36	..	4 16	4 41	..	7 11	..	8 51	..
3½	Nancegollan	....	8H 3	8 2	....	10H 2	....	10H36	....	12H11	....	1 22	....	3 43	....	4 25	4 48	....	7 18	....	8 58	....
6	Praze	..	8H 9	8 8	..	10H 9	..	10H42	..	12H17	..	1 29	..	3 49	..	4 30	4 55	..	7 25	..	9 4	..
8¾	**Gwinear Road** ..... arr	6 6	8 17	8 16	....	10 17	....	10 50	....	12 25	....	1 36	....	3 57	....	4 38	5 5	....	7 32	....	9 12	....

B Does not apply on August Bank Holiday. E Except Saturdays. H Passengers travelling by this train on Saturdays beyond Plymouth are required to hold Regulation Tickets (see pages 51, 52 and 53). S Saturdays only.
¶ By "Western National" Omnibus. Heavy luggage not conveyed. Connecting services are also run between Helston Station and Mullion Cove, etc.

Above: The Helston branch Summer Timetable, 18 June-9 September 1962. The Alterations Supplement for this period indicated that the 9.50pm service from Gwinear Road ran to such times on Saturdays only (SO) but departed on Monday to Friday (MF) at 9.30, to arrive at Helston at 9.55pm.

Below: The branch Winter Working Timetable, 10 September-3 November 1962.

WEEKDAYS **GWINEAR ROAD AND HELSTON**

SINGLE LINE—Worked by Electric Train Staff. Crossing Places, Nancegollan and Helston.
The speed of trains over the Branch not to exceed 35 miles per hour.

Mileage from Gwinear Road and Mile Post Mileage M	C	DOWN	Ruling Gradient 1 in	B		B	B		G	B	B	B	B	B	
				Mixed					LE						
				2C61	‡—Nancegollan, 8.2 a.m. ‡—Helston, 8.20 a.m. LE 5‖30 a.m. from Long Rock	2C61	2C6J	When necessary may convey trucks of grain traffic for Helston received on 7.50 p.m. Avonmouth Freight	0B31	2C61	2C61	2C61	2C61	2C61	
				am		am	am		Q PM	PM	PM	PM	PM	PM	
—	—	**GWINEAR ROAD** .. dep	—	7 45		8 30	10 55		12‖10	2 10	4 11	5 0	7 45	9 25	..
2	68	Praze	60R	7 55		8 38	11 3		......	2 18	4 19	5 8	7 53	9 33	......
5	10	Nancegollan .. .. .. arr	60F	8X2		8 43	11 8		..	2X23	4X24	5X13	7 58	9 38	..
		.... dep		8‡ 5		8 44	11 9		......	2 26	4 27	5 14	7 59	9 39	......
7	0	Truthall Platform	54F	..		8 50	11 15		..	2 32	4 33	5 20	..	9 45	..
8	67	**HELSTON** .... arr	61F	8‡15		8 55	11 20		12‖35	2 37	4 38	5 25	8 9	9 50	......

WEEKDAYS **HELSTON AND GWINEAR ROAD**

Mileage from Helston M	C	UP	Ruling Gradient 1 in	B	B	C	B		B	B	B	B				
				Mixed		Perishable					Mixed					
				2C61	2C61	3C21	2C61		2C61	2C61	2C61	2C61				
				★	★	★	★	Must not be delayed. Working to be given special attention	★	★	★	★				
				am	am	Q am	PM		PM	PM	PM	PM				
—	—	**HELSTON** .. .. .. dep	—	7 45	9 50	11 25	1 15		3 30	4 10	7 3	8 45	..	..	..	..
1	67	Truthall Platform	61R	7 52	......	......	......		3 37	4 17	7 10	8 50	......	......	......	......
3	57	Nancegollan .. .. .. arr	54R	7X58	10 1	11 36	1X26		3 43	4X23	7 16	8 58	..	..	..	..
		.... dep		8 3	10 4	11 41	1 29		3 44	4 25½	7 17	8 59	......	......	......	......
5	79	Praze	60R	8 9	10 10	11 47	1 35		3 50	4a31	7 23	9 5	..	..	..	..
8	67	**GWINEAR ROAD** arr	60F	8 16	10 17	11 54	1 42		3 57	4 38	7 30	9 12	......	......	......	......

Above: As there had been no Sunday services on the branch since at least 1920, the last trains ran on Saturday 3 November 1962. This was a day of heavy showers and sunny periods, as evidenced by this photograph of No D6308 entering the platform at Helston from the south, having collected its coaches from the end of the line to form the 4.10pm departure. This train would meet the 4.11pm service from Gwinear Road at Nancegollan and would carry out there the last ever passenger train crossing movement on the branch. *Author*

Below: Earlier in the day No D6336 – carrying the correct 2C61 headcode on the last day when it would be relevant – awaits departure with the 9.45am to Gwinear Road. This would be the last train from which passengers would be able to change at Gwinear Road to connect into the up 'Cornish Riviera Express'. *Author*

The very last passenger train from Helston was the 8.45pm, hauled by No D6312, which can just be discerned in this photograph taken from the first coach as it heads towards the Church Hill overbridge. *Helston Museum*

Right and below right: At Gwinear Road, before the locomotive ran round its six-coach train, No D6312 was photographed again. Its running-round manoeuvre, which involved running wrong line up the down main, was probably being delayed until after the departure of the 2.30pm from Paddington, due at Gwinear Road between 9.19 and 9.20. Two young boys, who will now be approaching the eligibility age for a Senior Railcard, look on with their parents in amazement at the mourners on the platform. The mourner carrying the axe represents Dr Beeching, and the billboard carries a farewell message from 'Old Helstonian Grammar School Train Boys', many of whom had used the line to get to and from school. A local solicitor carried a 'For Sale' board. *Helston Museum*

Opposite top: On its return journey to Helston, the cab of No D6312 was a popular spot! Among the 'guests' was Dr Michael, a Helston doctor who had for many years been the railway employees' first aid instructor, and his daughter. A crowd awaits the arrival of the train. *Western Morning News*

Opposite bottom After the passengers had left the train, all assembled on the platform for a photograph staged by the local press. The happy smiles and waves, no doubt requested by the photographer, belie the sadness of the occasion. The author is amongst the crowd. *Author's collection*

The freight only period

SPECIAL ROAD SERVICES
BETWEEN
CAMBORNE/REDRUTH
AND
HELSTON (Cornwall)
ON
SATURDAYS ONLY—JUNE 22nd to SEPTEMBER 7th, inclusive, 1963

This page: In reaching its conclusion to approve the withdrawal of passenger services, the TUCC had taken into account the promise by the BTC 'to provide extra buses to connect with trains ... on Saturdays throughout the summer when tourist traffic is especially heavy'. Such buses were provided, at least between 22 June and 7 September 1963, connecting with ten up services and nine down services at Camborne, and with the up and down 'Cornish Riviera Express' at Redruth. I do not know how far these leaflets were distributed, and how many passengers took advantage of the facility, especially as all connections involved a wait of no less than 35 minutes. Similar special road services were provided between Truro and St Agnes & Perranporth, following the closure of the branch between Chacewater and Newquay in February 1963. *Author's collection*

Opposite page: Freight trains to Helston lingered on for slightly under two further years. Even in 1962 there remained healthy freight traffic on the branch, but carried in 10-ton vans and open wagons at costs (whether to the customer or more probably to British Railways) that were unsustainable in the context of increasingly competitive road transport. Traffic is healthy, but still probably not profitable, in these goods-only era photographs of No D6307 in the yard and from the cab of D6325. Passenger services having been withdrawn and the engine shed no longer being in use, goods trains could now use the platform line; the engine shed spur plays host to stone traffic hopper wagons. *Both author*

ON SATURDAYS ONLY during the above period special road services will operate from and to CAMBORNE station for the exclusive use of passengers holding through single and ordinary return tickets to HELSTON via Camborne.

One special road service will operate similarly on these SATURDAYS in each direction between REDRUTH and HELSTON to connect with the "Cornish Riviera" Express (From Paddington: Redruth arrive 5.3 p.m.; To Paddington: Redruth depart 10.42 a.m.).

Details of the timetable for these special buses are shown overleaf.

PROVISION WILL BE MADE ON THE SPECIAL BUSES FOR
PASSENGERS' ACCOMPANIED LUGGAGE

Passengers in possession of through rail tickets to Helston, arriving at Camborne or Redruth stations on the SATURDAYS referred to at times not covered by the special bus service will have their tickets honoured on the Western National Omnibus Company's existing stage carriage services—heavy luggage NOT conveyed—and should travel as under:

Camborne–Helston by Western National Omnibus Company Service No. 30.
Redruth–Helston by Western National Omnibus Company Service No. 31.

All passengers travelling beyond Plymouth from Camborne and Redruth by certain trains on Saturdays during the Summer Train Service are required to obtain a Special REGULATION TICKET, issued without charge, which ensures a seat on the train.

Regulation Tickets can be obtained in advance at any station or ticket agency on production of a valid rail ticket to cover the journey not later than three weeks prior to date of travel after which Regulation Tickets may be obtained on personal application at HELSTON, CAMBORNE or REDRUTH railway stations.

Further details of the special Seat Regulation Arrangements from West Cornwall Stations can be obtained from stations or ticket agencies.

Facilities are available at Helston station to deal with parcels traffic, including "Passengers' Luggage in Advance" arrangements, and the issue of rail tickets.

SEND YOUR LUGGAGE IN ADVANCE

S. E. RAYMOND, General Manager.

R1417   Printed by Latimer, Trend & Co. Ltd., Plymouth

BRITISH RAILWAYS (WESTERN REGION)
THE WESTERN NATIONAL OMNIBUS COMPANY LIMITED

Timetable of SPECIAL JOURNEYS for passengers holding THROUGH BOOKED RAIL TICKETS ONLY

CAMBORNE/REDRUTH — HELSTON

SATURDAYS ONLY—JUNE 22nd to SEPTEMBER 7th, inclusive, 1963

	a.m.	a.m.	a.m.	p.m.	p.m.	p.m.	p.m.	p.m.	p.m.	p.m.	p.m.
Redruth (Railway Station) .. .. .. dep.	—	—	—	—	—	—	—	—	5 25	—	—
Camborne (Railway Station)	7 40	8 35	10 50	12 0	1 35	2 25	3 5	4 35	—	7 0	—
Helston (Western National Garage, Clodgey Lane) .. .. .. arr.	8 15	9 10	11 25	12 35	2 10	3 0	3 40	5 10	6 0	7 35	—

	a.m.	a.m.	a.m.	a.m.	p.m.	p.m.	p.m.	p.m.	p.m.	p.m.	p.m.
Helston (Western National Garage, Clodgey Lane) .. .. .. dep.	9 30	10 0	10 50	11 45	1 25	2 20	3 50	4 15	5 30	6 10	7 40
Camborne (Railway Station)	—	10 35	11 25	12 20	2 0	2 55	4 25	4 50	6 5	6 45	8 15
Redruth (Railway Station) .. .. .. arr.	10 5	—	—	—	—	—	—	—	—	—	—

* One special bus service in each direction between Redruth and Helston connecting with the "Cornish Riviera" Expresses.
(From Paddington: Redruth arrive 5.4 p.m.; To Paddington: Redruth depart 10.40 a.m.).

British Railways (Western Region)

Plymouth Division

PUBLIC NOTICE

The Railways Board hereby give notice that on and from Monday, 5th October, 1964, freight wagon load facilities will be withdrawn from Helston, Nancegollan and Praze stations, the Gwinear Road to Helston branch line freight train service withdrawn and the branch closed. Praze station will be closed and parcels facilities withdrawn from Nancegollan.

Existing arrangements for the collection and/or delivery of parcels and freight sundries traffic in the area will be maintained. Orders for collections should be sent to the following :-

HELSTON AREA
Goods Agent, Penzance

NANCEGOLLAN & PRAZE AREA
Goods Agent, Redruth, Drump Lane

Facilities for the handing in and/or collection of such traffic by the public will continue to be available at Helston.

The alternative station for freight wagon loads, also parcels traffic will be as follows :-

DESCRIPTION OF TRAFFIC	HELSTON TRAFFIC	NANCEGOLLAN & PRAZE TRAFFIC
GENERAL MERCHANDISE	Penzance	Redruth, Drump Lane
COAL CLASS TRAFFIC	Carn Brea, Station Yard Sidings	Carn Brea, Station Yard Sidings
PARCELS	Helston, as now	Camborne, Gwinear Road or Helston

Traffic not requiring Railway cartage facilities could be consigned from or to other retained freight stations in the area.

Full cartage services will be available to traders at Penzance and Redruth, Drump Lane.

Above: Two goods trains ran each way on the branch on Monday to Friday, with one service on Saturday. The branch remained fully signalled, the signal boxes at both Helston and Nancegollan remained open, and staff costs will have remained high. The doubtful economics of this exercise are personified by this 1963 photograph of D6326 arriving at Helston with a guard's van and no commercial traffic whatever. *Author*

Left: In contrast to passenger services, goods services could be withdrawn without public consultation or the involvement of the TUCC. Formal posters were not produced, and the announcement of the withdrawal of freight facilities was contained in a simple, typed and undated notice. Reports in the local newspaper indicate that the notice was published in late July or early August without any prior notice having been given to Helston Borough Council. *Author's collection*

Opposite bottom: This photograph is a mystery. The stonework and the gradient of the road above clearly identify this to be the Helston side of the Church Hill over bridge. Work has commenced to fill in the cutting to enable Station Road to be extended, but the pipe does not appear to feature in any earlier photograph. Perhaps it was previously buried under the trackbed. *Helston Museum*

Demolition

Above: Assurances were given by the Parliamentary Secretary to the Minister of Transport to Helston Borough Council in December 1964 that the track would not be removed without the prior approval of the Minister, and the Borough Council was promised that it would be given prior warning if any application for consent .was to be made to the Minister. In April 1964 the Mayor announced that such promise had been broken, and demolition work commenced that month. Track removal commenced at the Helston end. Although the station building, goods shed, signal box, engine shed and signals remain in place, the track at the terminus has already been cut up into small lengths to facilitate its removal by road. *Osborne Studios, Helston*

Left: At Nancegollan longer lengths of track – perhaps intended for use elsewhere – are loaded onto a motor lorry. *The late Fred Ivey*

The track has gone, but it is still protected by the bracket signal for the engine shed and the main line (probably dating from 1915), the small shunting signals, and the modern Advance Starter and Home signals on either side of the Church Hill overbridge. *The late Fred Ivey*

Right: Until the HRPS commenced running limited services on its restored line, this must have been the last railway vehicle to operate on the branch. At the very end of the remaining line, an inspection trolley oversees the destruction of the track and its removal by road vehicle at Faulls Crossing, between Praze and Nancegollan. *The late Fred Ivey*

Branch motive power

Below: No details are known of the locomotive that hauled the inaugural train in 1887 (page 24), but it appears to have been a 0-6-0ST. During the early years it is believed that motive power on the branch included 0-6-0STs of Classes '2021' and '850'; Class '517' 0-4-2Ts; 'Metro' Class 2-4-0Ts; and the unusual 0-4-4Ts, No 34 and 35. Part of No 35 can be seen in the photograph on page 82, but this is a wonderful, if posed, portrait of its sister locomotive No 34, believed to have been taken at St Ives in about 1905. The staff are, and are entitled to be, proud of the immaculate appearance of the locomotive. These two locomotives were originally built at Swindon as 0-4-2Ts in 1890 but were rebuilt as 0-4-4Ts in 1895, then used extensively on the Helston and St Ives lines.

Opposite top: Class '850' 0-6-0ST No 1971 features in this clear (and again posed) photograph of the train and staff in Helston. The locomotive is at the head of two Brake Composites, believed to have been built in 1895 and probably the first bogie coaches on the branch. It is known that Class '850' locomotives operated on the line in the late 1890s. No 1971 was recorded on the nearby St Ives branch in July 1897, and No 1973 on the Helston branch during the following month. The saddle tanks were later rebuilt by the GWR as pannier tanks, but there is no evidence of their use in rebuilt form on the branch. *Helston Museum*

Opposite bottom: Use of 'Metro' 2-4-0Ts is evidenced by this photograph of No 1496 alongside the goods shed at Helston. *Helston Museum*

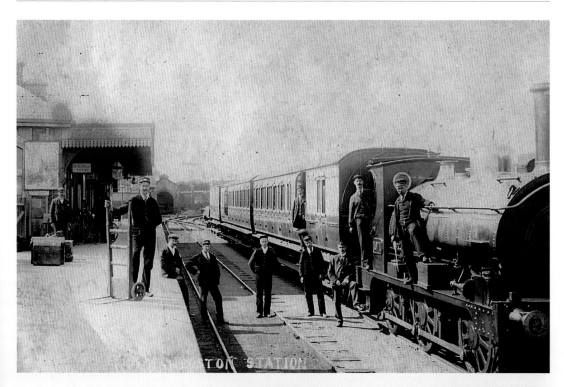

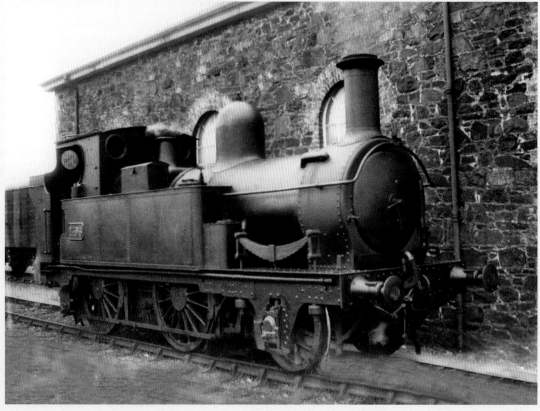

Above: No 4406 was photographed at Penzance. It was allocated to Helston, St Ives and Penzance between 1928 and 1931 and again in 1932. Every member of the class was shedded at some time at Helston, St Ives or Penzance and is likely to have visited Helston. Sister engine No 3102 (4402) was allocated to Helston when new on delivery from Wolverhampton Works. *David Collings collection, Lens of Sutton*

Below: Class '44XX' locomotives were introduced and shared duties with the smaller engines and steam railmotors before the First World War, but surprisingly few photographs seem to have been taken of these locomotives on the line.

Under the GWR renumbering scheme of December 1912, the locomotives were renumbered from 115/3101-3110 to 4400-4410 respectively. An early print of an unidentified member of the class with its original small coal bunker was published in the October 1911 issue of *The Railway Magazine*, and Peter Treloar unearthed this undated postcard of No 4404 in Helston station. By that date the locomotive had been renumbered and rebuilt with a larger bunker. Behind it may be one of the ventilated goods vans used for regular rabbit traffic from Helston to Sheffield. No 4404 was allocated to Helston, St Ives and Penzance for most of the time between 1926 and 1934. *P. Q. Treloar collection*

Below: Also rarely photographed on the branch, and indeed not referred to in some writings about it, were the Class '48XX' (later '14XX') 0-4-2Ts briefly tested by the GWR when new in the 1930s. They bore an uncanny resemblance to the Class '517s' built between 1868 and 1885, and as these had been used on the Helston branch it was perhaps not surprising that the new class should be tested at Helston.

Above: No 4868 is seen here at the head of an equally new 'B set' on 10 June 1936, and shunting at Helston. It had been allocated to Exeter shed when new in early 1936, and it is reasonable to assume that it may have been loaned to Penzance shed for trials on the Helston line later in the year. *G. N. Southerden, the late Alan Jackson collection/Kidderminster Railway Museum*

No 4868 is seen again shunting at Helston in June 1936. The Starter signal has been lowered to allow it to move towards Church Hill bridge, but neither the Advance Starter nor the shunting signal has been cleared. *G. N. Southerden, the late Alan Jackson collection*

At the Lizard, Cornwall.

TRANSPORT TRUST

GWR ROAD
MOTOR SERVICES

The Lizard to Helston Station
bus service inaugurated in August 1903
was the first railway-operated motor
bus service in the UK

For further information visit
www.transporttrust.com

TRANSPORT HERITAGE SITE

Far right: A GWR poster advertising the Road Motor Service for the period 24 January-30 April 1924. *Author's collection*

Right: An original bus ticket. *Colin Billington's Collection*

This photograph, which has not to my knowledge been published previously, shows Milnes-Daimler No 9 (AF 141) in Godolphin Road heading towards the centre of Helston. The bus is (at best) in the middle of the road, if not actually on the right-hand side! Except for the street lights, this scene is almost unchanged today. The water channels – 'kennels' – between the road and the pavement are a feature of many streets in Helston. *Helston Museum*

The GWR continued to operate buses in Cornwall until its services were taken over from 1 January 1929 by the Western National Omnibus Company Limited, a newly formed company in which the GWR held a 50% interest. A vehicle purchased by the GWR in 1927, and believed to be the only ex-GWR bus to survive, is Guy FBB No 1268 (YF 714), which spent much of its life at Penzance bus depot and may well have operated to Helston and even to The Lizard. No 1268 has been lovingly restored by Colin Billington, and is seen here shortly after restoration was completed in 2010. *Colin Billington*

Above, below and opposite top: In 1953 the 50th anniversary of the historic GWR bus service was celebrated by British Railways (Western Region) when a bronze plaque was unveiled at Helston station by Mr A. E. C. Dent, Executive Officer for Road Motor Engineering at the Railway Executive, in the presence of the Mayor of Helston, local dignitaries and many former employees associated with the service. Prior to the demolition of the station building the plaque was presented to Helston Museum. *Author/Philip J. Kelley collection (2)*

THIS TABLET COMMEMORATES THE OPENING OF THE FIRST RAILWAY MOTOR OMNIBUS SERVICE WHICH WAS RUN BY THE GREAT WESTERN RAILWAY FROM HELSTON TO THE LIZARD 17 TH. AUGUST. 1903

Opposite: After the ceremony, and as on similar occasions in the past relating to the railway, the party adjourned to the Angel Hotel for a celebratory five-course lunch. This menu was signed by many of the dignitaries as a memento of the day. *Author's collection*

BRITISH RAILWAYS
Western Region.

J. A. Pascoe, Mayor of Helston

JUBILEE

OF FIRST RAILWAY MOTOR OMNIBUS SERVICE WHICH
WAS INAUGURATED BY THE GREAT WESTERN RAILWAY
BETWEEN HELSTON AND THE LIZARD.

MONDAY, 17th AUGUST, 1903.

ANGEL HOTEL, HELSTON.
MONDAY, 17th AUGUST, 1953.

MENU.

Creme Portugaise.

—

Filet de Sole Frite. Sauce Tartare.

—

Agneau Roti. Sauce Menthe.

Haricots Verts. Carottes au Beurre.

Pommes Persillees

—

Coupe Jacques. Cornish Cream.

—

Fromage et Biscuits.

—

Cafe.

Above: During the Western National era, from November 1932 buses were operated from from a new purpose-built garage in Clodgey Lane, Helston, on or close to the proposed route of the light railway. From the immaculate appearance of Bristol KS6B No 1810 (LTA 829) heading for The Lizard on Route 27, and the two-way traffic in Meneage Street in Helston, it is possible to date this photograph to 1951 or 1952. Even though traffic in the early 1950s was light by modern standards, it is clear from this photograph that traffic congestion in the narrow streets of Cornish towns was already a serious problem. *Colin Billington collection*

Right: Helston bus garage operated both double-decker and single-decker buses on the Lizard peninsula, as illustrated in this view of WN Bristol B35R No 105 (FJ 8935) arriving at Helston station on Route 29 from Gillan Wartha. The service to Manaccan had been extended to Gillan by the GWR in September 1928, only shortly before the transfer of bus services to Western National. No 105 had been delivered new to Western National in 1933, but was given a new Beadle body in June 1950, which still looks very smart a year or two later. On the left, and partly obscuring the station platform and goods shed, stands newly delivered No 1811, probably awaiting its turn on a service to The Lizard (Route 27/27A) or Kuggar

(Route 26). Nos 1810/11 always looked a little odd because they were built with 8-foot-wide bodies on 7ft 6in chassis after the Ministry of Transport permitted wider vehicles. The apparently inset wheels can be seen on No 1811. *Colin Billington collection*

The 75th anniversary of the bus service in 1978 was also celebrated, by which time Western National was part of the nationalised National Bus Company (NBC), created by the Labour Government under Harold Wilson. Under NBC control, the route number changed to 527. To mark the anniversary the superintendent of the Western National depot in Helston liaised with the Cornwall Vintage Vehicle Society to organise a cavalcade of old vehicles – including for part of the way a horse-drawn Jersey car – and Western National arranged for a double-decker to be repainted in GWR chocolate and cream livery with appropriate advertisements. Strangely, the chosen vehicle was not an ex-Western National bus, but ex-Devon General Atlantean No 900 (900 DTT), but it would be churlish to complain about the result as it stands in all its glory outside The Top House at The Lizard. *Author's collection*

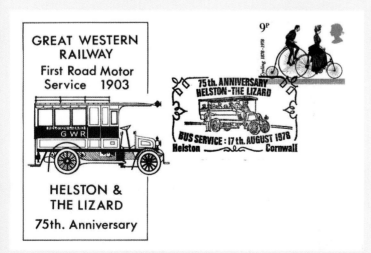

A 'first-day cover' produced to celebrate the event. *Author's collection*

Bus privatisation

After the Transport Act 1985 introduced competition to the bus market and former NBC subsidiaries were sold out of public ownership, the service to The Lizard was operated by a number of different companies. For about 15 years Truronian operated a number of routes in the Helston area, and in 2003 the centenary of the GWR bus service was celebrated. Again Western National (by now part of First Group after it had been purchased from the NBC) arranged for a double-decker to be painted in GWR livery, and this time Bristol VR No 1003 (VDV 141S) was chosen. On 17 August 2003 a cavalcade of buses again drove to The Lizard, headed by No 1003 seen here alongside the remains of the platform at Helston station, and turning into Godolphin Road from Station Road; the author (wearing his Traffic Commissioner yellow jacket) can be seen waving from the top deck. Brand new Truronian Dennis Dart TTO3 TRU follows. *Author, author's collection*

Below left and right: After Truronian was taken over by First Devon & Cornwall (the name given to the former Western National some time after First Group purchased the company from NBC), First again operated the service to The Lizard for a short period. It was then operated by Western Greyhound, one of whose vehicles No. 557 (WK04 BUS) was photographed at The Lizard on 2 February 2012.

However, following a re-tendering exercise carried throughout the county by Cornwall Council at the end of 2011, First Devon & Cornwall recovered the route at the end of March 2012. No doubt on a driver training exercise, First's Optaire No. 53403 (TL54 TVL) was also photographed at The Lizard in March alongside the signpost directing visitors to Britain's most southerly point. The Top House (formerly Hill's Hotel) can be seen in the background in both photographs. *Author/First Devon & Cornwall*

Above: To mark the occasion a water-colour of early buses at Helston station was painted by Ken Mortimer. No doubt with some artistic licence, it features one of the cars used at the opening of the service and, behind, a 20hp Dennis, which dates from about 1911. Whether these vehicles ever met together at Helston matters not – the painting creates a wonderful evocation of an historic experiment. *Author's copyright*

Left: Also souvenir reproduction tickets were produced for the day.

This photograph taken in Coinagehall Street in Helston on 25 February 2008 is particularly interesting because it shows not only Truronian Dennis Dart T32 JCV on The Lizard-Helston-St Agnes Route T1, but also T34 JCV on Truronian's route T34 between Helston and Redruth. This service was marketed as 'The Helston Branch Line', and the bus services were specifically timed to make connections with London trains. *Author*

After Truronian was taken over by First Devon & Cornwall (the new name given to Western National some time after First Group purchased the company from NBC), First again operated the service for a short period, but it is then operated by Western Greyhound. One of that company's new Optare vehicles, No 988 (WK11 APZ), is seen in Coinagehall Street on 28 August 2011. Following a re-tendering excercise, from April 2012 the route is again operated by First Devon & Cornwall Ltd. *Western Greyhound*

After the abortive reopening scheme in 1994, it was not until 2001 that the two founder members of the Helston Railway Preservation Society (HRPS) – James Packman and Perry McDonagh – came up with the idea of trying to reopen part of the branch as a tourist attraction. Other supporters are seen standing in front of Trevarno Bridge at about the same time. It took a lot of optimism, the prospect of much hard work and the invaluable support of the Trevarno Estate to contemplate any restoration of any part of the line in these conditions. *Stuart Walker*

Once the undergrowth had been removed and the former trackbed revealed, the members could see the results of their efforts, and there were grounds for cautious optimism. In this view it is now obvious that a railway ran along here, and a new station on this site can realistically be envisaged. *Stuart Walker*

Inset above: Within two years the trackbed near Trevarno had been cleared in preparation for the laying of the first piece of track. The official ceremony took place in the presence of the Mayor of Helston on Bank Holiday Monday, 7 May 2007, unfortunately in very wet conditions.

However, the weather on the previous day was dry and bright, when volunteers were photographed preparing the first length of track for the official ceremony. The proposed site for the new station at Trevarno lies on the right beyond the bridge. *Author*

Inset right: Even before any track had been laid, some members were considering what vehicles could be used on the reinstated line. As early as the spring of 2006 a two-car Park Royal DMU had been purchased by the Helston Railway Diesel Group from the West Somerset Railway. The Class 103 unit was delivered in May to

Gwinear Road, where it was photographed on 6 June 2006 when temporarily berthed in the former cattle dock with the kind permission of the owners of the former station master's house. When new in 1957 the unit (Nos W50413 and W56159) operated in the Birmingham area before being transferred to the Plymouth division. *Author*

Above: By September 2007 track-laying had progressed sufficiently for the DMU to be transferred to Trevarno, where it was joined by two Ruston & Hornsby 0-4-0 diesel-mechanical shunters from the Northampton Ironstone Railway. No 395305 was, and remains, painted black ('the black diesel') and is seen here on arrival at Trevarno. It was restored to working order in February 2011, and has been very active since. *Alan Burton*

Left: The other shunter – R&H No 327947 – is now painted blue ('the blue diesel'). It was originally delivered to the British Sugar Corporation in Banbury in 1954, and was later transferred to that company's works in Kings Lynn. Withdrawn in 1997, it was sold to the Northampton Railway Trust. Although never owned or operated by British Railways, it was delivered to Trevarno carrying the fictitious number D2959 and early BR emblem; this can be explained by the fact that two shunters of a similar design (Nos 11507/08 – later D2957/58) were in BR stock between 1956 and 1967. As D2959, the shunter was photographed at Trevarno being off-loaded on to the line. *Alan Burton*

Above: A year later, on 9 May 2009, D2959 has been repainted in BR blue and renumbered 97649, again a fictitious number in the BR departmental series. It is seen here preparing to shunt the DMU into the new bay at Trevarno on the left. *Author*

Left: For the first time since 1962, over the weekend of 25/26 July 2010 steam returned to the line, by which time the new platform at Trevarno had been completed. Ex-Par Docks 0-4-0ST *Judy* was hired from the Bodmin & Wenford Railway for the occasion. *Author*

The completed platform can be seen crowded with spectators as *Judy* approaches from Gansey Farm, near Prospidnick Bridge, on 25 July. In the background of this photograph, taken from the footplate, can be seen the new footbridge at Tregadjack erected by the HRPS to carry a public footpath over the restored line. *Author*

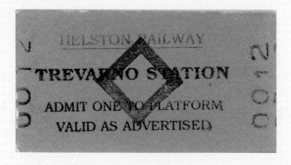

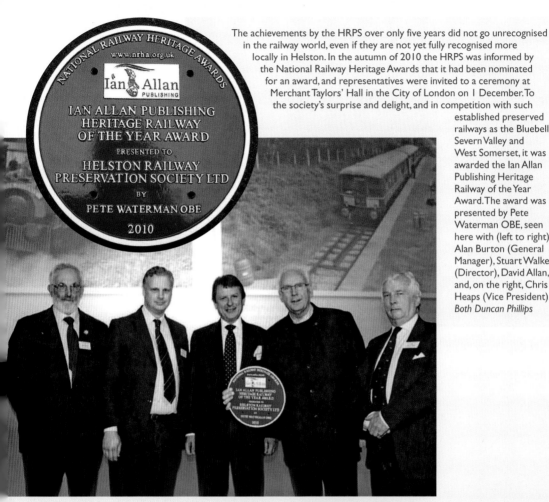

The achievements by the HRPS over only five years did not go unrecognised in the railway world, even if they are not yet fully recognised more locally in Helston. In the autumn of 2010 the HRPS was informed by the National Railway Heritage Awards that it had been nominated for an award, and representatives were invited to a ceremony at Merchant Taylors' Hall in the City of London on 1 December. To the society's surprise and delight, and in competition with such established preserved railways as the Bluebell, Severn Valley and West Somerset, it was awarded the Ian Allan Publishing Heritage Railway of the Year Award. The award was presented by Pete Waterman OBE, seen here with (left to right) Alan Burton (General Manager), Stuart Walker (Director), David Allan, and, on the right, Chris Heaps (Vice President). *Both Duncan Phillips*

In May 2011 the railway was visited by David Allan and John Ellis, a former General Manager of Scotrail and chairman of the judges for the awards. On the platform at Trevarno are (left to right) Ken Wood (President), Stuart Walker, Matthew Laughter (HRPS volunteer), David Allan and John Ellis. The 'black diesel', repainted since 2008 but still not carrying any number, stands on the right preparing to give the guests a ride on the line. *Richard Barnes*

2nd · SINGLE   SINGLE · 2nd
Helston to
Helston   Helston
Truthall Bridge Ht   Truthall Bridge Ht
TRUTHALL BRIDGE HALT
(W)   5d. Fare 5d.   (W)
For conditions see over For conditions see over

During the second half of 2011 the trackbed has been cleared and ballast laid in preparation for an extension and in early 2012, track laying continued to the south towards Truthall Halt. Planning permission has been obtained to build a replica of the GWR 'pagoda' shelter at Truthall Halt, the site of which lies to the right of the point to which track had been laid by 6 March 2012. This is south of the point that enables HRPS to claim that the Helston Railway again operates the most southerly railway in Great Britain. The pedestrian footbridge constructed by HRPS to the south of Trevarno can be seen in the top left hand corner of the photograph. *Author/Alan Burton*

The HRPS carried its first fare-paying passengers during Trevarno Winter Wonderland celebrations between 17 and 21 December 2011, when more than 1,000 passengers travelled in the society's restored brake-van hauled by the 'black diesel' over the full length of the current line. The restored and repainted diesel is seen here at Trevarno preparing to haul the brake-van on one of the first passenger-carrying services on the restored line. This augurs well for celebrations in the branch's 125th anniversary year in 2012, by the end of which track should have been laid as far as Truthall Halt. *Barbara Barnes*

Helston Museum

elston Museum is situated in the very centre of the town and close to the Guildhall. It must be one of the best local museums in the country, and contains an interesting transport section. As can be seen in this recent photograph, the museum houses many exhibits referred to in this book, including the spade and wheelbarrow used at the ceremony of cutting the first sod on the railway, the poster advertising that ceremony, the statutory closure notice, a cabside number plate from Class '45XX' No 4566, and a presentation nameplate marking the naming of Virgin Cross Country HST power car No 43103 after the Furry Dance. The cabinet on the right contains the Helston-Nancegollan Crossing and Nancegollan Crossing-Gwinear Road staffs issued by signalmen to authorise trains to enter those parts of the line. *Author's collection*

The future

Above: What of the future? It is the long-term ambition of the HRPS to reopen the line over the Cober Viaduct to the outskirts of Helston, to a location on the edge of the Water-ma-Trout Industrial Estate near the Lowertown road bridges. Given the successes of the last ten years, this must be an achievable objective, but the scale of the task is demonstrated by this photograph taken looking towards Helston from the overbridge at Truthall Halt in May 2007. Somewhere beneath the rhododendron bushes, trees and scrub is a trackbed! *Author*

Right: It would be wrong to end on anything but a positive note. This photograph of new track heading towards Helston under the new footbridge constructed by the HRPS shows what can be achieved. *Barbara Barnes*

Can you help? If you are interested in joining the Helston Railway Preservation Society and supporting the rebuilding of the railway, please contact the Hon Membership Secretary, Barbara Barnes, at Clowance Barton Lodge, Praze-an-Beeble, Camborne, Cornwall TR14 0PR, or by e-mail at

membership@helstonrailway.co.uk.